"For many years I've been seeking a way to be centered and calm during the stressful moments that often fill my busy days. Each time I've tried something, I am hopeful at first, but then I am often disappointed by the lack of results over time. So it has been a wonderful surprise and delight that Dr. Felder's easy-to-use book has given me a new level of calm and strength that I've never known. This book is a gift; the effectiveness of these mindfulness methods have continued to help me day after day, long after I first explored the chapters and tried out the sacred remedies he describes."

—Connie Goldman, award-winning producer and writer for National Public Radio

"*Here I Am* is a very enjoyable and valuable guide that shows how Jewish spirituality can help us cope with those moments of intense stress that are part of every life. I am particularly grateful that so much wisdom has been gathered together in one place in this book, and I will be recommending *Here I Am* to many people and with much enthusiasm!"

—Rabbi Sally J. Priesand, first ordained woman rabbi

"*Here I Am* is a breath of restorative fresh air. Breathe it in. I've used Dr. Felder's incredibly practical ideas to find calm amidst the everyday storms."

—David Nathan Weiss, Oscar-nominated screenwriter of *Shrek 2*

Here I Am

*Using Jewish Spiritual Wisdom to
Become More Present, Centered,
and Available for Life*

LEONARD FELDER, PhD

TRUMPETER • *Boston* • 2011

Trumpeter Books
An imprint of Shambhala Publications, Inc.
Horticultural Hall
300 Massachusetts Avenue
Boston, Massachusetts 02115
trumpeterbooks.com

9 8 7 6 5 4 3 2 1

First Edition
Printed in the United States of America

♾This edition is printed on acid-free paper that meets the
American National Standards Institute z39.48 Standard.
♻This book is printed on 30% postconsumer recycled paper.
For more information please visit us at www.shambhala.com.

Distributed in the United States by Random House, Inc.,
and in Canada by Random House of Canada Ltd

Designed by James D. Skatges

Library of Congress Cataloging-in-Publication Data
Felder, Leonard.
Here I am: using Jewish spiritual wisdom to become more present,
centered, and available for life/Leonard Felder.
p.   cm.
Includes bibliographical references and index.
ISBN 978-1-59030-844-8 (pbk.: alk. paper)
1. Self-actualization (Psychology) 2. Self-actualization
(Psychology)—Religious aspects—Judaism. 3. Stress management.
4. Spiritual life—Judaism. 5. Self-help techniques. I. Title.
BF637.S4F427 2011
296.7—dc22
2011000480

For my niece Erica Helene Ruff who is a bit curious about Jewish spirituality.

I hope this book will help you nourish your beautiful soul and deal with the many daily stresses in your life.

Contents

Author's Note

Sometimes in this book you will see Hebrew words that may be unfamiliar. Please don't worry. I will spell them out phonetically in English, and you can sound them out as they appear on the page.

The only confusing words are those that contain *ch*. For instance, the word *Shechinah* is a mystical term that refers to the indwelling Presence of the Divine (which some scholars call the feminine aspect of the One). Rather than saying this word with a "ch" sound as in "chew" or "child," you instead use a clearing-your-throat sound, as when you say the familiar words *chutzpah* (bold nerve or entitlement), *challah* (the special braided bread for the Sabbath), or *li'chayim* (as in "to life, to life, li'chayim" from *Fiddler on the Roof*).

If you aren't comfortable yet making the "ch" sound as described here, please don't sweat it. You can pronounce any unfamiliar words in your own style and still benefit enormously from the techniques and insights contained in these eight chapters.

Here I Am

Introduction

EVERY SO OFTEN, it's a good idea to sit down and ask yourself, "How am I going to improve the way I deal with the pressures, complexities, and stressful moments that are now an undeniable part of my life?"

Such a question doesn't mean that you've been doing something terribly wrong or that you need to turn your entire life upside down to improve things. Rather, it's about being honest with yourself and looking for realistic ways to be healthier, more centered, and more effective in your work and personal life. It's about asking the right questions and coming up with the most satisfying and effective solutions. For example, you can start by trying to answer the following questions:

- Is my daily schedule more demanding and overloaded than it used to be?

- Do I feel that I'm usually rushing faster or trying harder but still falling behind?

- Do I sometimes feel pulled and twisted, like a frayed rubber band on the verge of snapping, because unresolved situations in my life are tugging at me with more and more intensity?

- Is it hard to find a balance between being extremely productive and having enough time and energy to enjoy the less driven, more intimate moments of life?

- Is there someone I care about deeply who is also feeling overstressed or unable to breathe because of too much recent pressure?

In the past few decades, many approaches, workshops, therapies, and books have been devoted to the topic of stress. Some of them are quite good, but they usually require that you make large investments of time and money, as well as major lifestyle changes, and that you follow a huge number of meticulous steps and procedures (for which most busy people don't have the time or patience).

Yet what if there were a well-tested solution available at no cost (and more important, with no bad side effects) for the numerous moments when you or a loved one experience a stressful day or must deal with frustrating delays, losses, or setbacks? What if there were a safe and effective method you could learn easily to boost your energy, increase your creativity, and regain your strong center at the crucial moments when you start to feel stressed or overloaded? What if you could make a huge, long-lasting improvement toward being less stressed while continuing to come through for your loved ones, to meet your many important responsibilities, and to participate in the creative and compassionate projects that mean so much to you?

This book describes eight easy-to-understand and extremely effective stress-reduction and mind-focusing methods that can dramatically improve how you deal with the pressures and challenges of your busy life. Most important, these remedies for stress don't require that you turn your life upside down or make drastic changes that go against what truly matters to you.

For almost thirty years, I've been researching and testing these eight remedies. In my private practice as a licensed psychologist, I meet smart and compassionate people every day who want to have more energy and strength; they want to find effective methods to handle the daily pressures from their jobs, their families, their physical health challenges, or their individual search for meaning and purpose. These men and women are looking for proven techniques that they can count on to provide rapid relief and renewed creativity, even in the middle of a frustrating, tension-filled day.

I first began looking into how to deal more effectively with stress and personal health challenges many years before I became a trained psychologist. At a relatively young age, I started to have physical symptoms from trying to do too much each day; I began to have severe stomach problems and painful back and neck issues. As my beloved grandma from the old country used to say, "Oy, don't ask. You don't want to know."

At that time, in my midtwenties, I began testing out various traditional and nontraditional remedies for healing the body and clarifying the mind at the moments when my life felt off track or overloaded. I hoped to find a reliable and easy way (with few or no side effects) to stay centered and healthy, especially during busy days and intense weeks.

Yet even though I completed my PhD in holistic psychology and explored several different approaches from various spiritual traditions for healing and wellness, I kept finding that the most effective and profound remedies for stress and overload came from a place I didn't expect—the world of Jewish spirituality. This source surprised me at first, because I had never been told as a child during twelve years of twice-a-week Hebrew school (or in either of the congregations where I was an active member) that my Jewish heritage contained such extraordinary tools and solutions for successfully navigating the stressful moments of modern life. But the more I learned over the next thirty years from various compassionate rabbis and scholars (and the more I tried out these particular methods in my own life and with my counseling clients), the more I realized that these remedies were reliable and extremely useful, especially for those of us who find ourselves juggling multiple responsibilities in our personal lives as well as high-pressure jobs.

While these eight remedies are from Jewish sources, I've found that they consistently result in substantial improvements in focus, health, and clarity for a wide variety of women and men from Jewish, Catholic, Protestant, Buddhist, Hindu, Muslim, Baha'i, Sikh, Religious Science, agnostic, and nonreligious backgrounds. You don't need to be a long-time student of meditation to benefit from these particular methods; among the therapy clients, friends, and colleagues who have become less stressed and more energized from using these techniques are many lawyers, accountants, engineers, writers, artists, actors, directors, marketing professionals, entrepreneurs, nonprofit executives, health professionals, rabbis, cantors, teachers, ministers, priests, teens, young adults, midlife adults, and elders—each of them dealing with a slightly different stressful situation.

What I find most helpful about these methods for stress reduction and refocusing is that they address not only the physical aspects of stress but also the deeply spiritual and personal questions that tend to arise when you constantly feel interrupted by too many challenging situations on a hectic day. As you have probably noticed in your own life, a particularly hectic moment involving numerous frustrations or complicated decisions can drain your physical and emotional energy and also disrupt your sense of overall well-being. You might find yourself asking, "Why is this happening to me?" "What is the lesson I'm supposed to be learning here?" or "How do I get back on track with my higher purpose instead of repeatedly feeling bogged down?"

I first began to see the benefits of combining traditional psychotherapy and an openness to these essentially spiritual questions many years ago when I studied with Dr. Viktor Frankl.[1] He was a Holocaust survivor and a trained physician from Vienna, Austria, whose books describe how he successfully helped numerous individuals in the concentration camps (and later, thousands of clients) to become more resilient, stronger, and healthier by focusing on the daily spiritual search to find deeper meaning and greater purpose even in the most difficult situations.

Instead of looking at people as "very neurotic" or "highly defective," Frankl discovered how to find and boost a person's inner courage, inner strength, and growing sense of personal dignity by focusing on how to reconnect with the highest self. He often said that "even in the toughest situations, the one freedom which no one can take away from you is the freedom to choose your spiritual attitude, to clarify your unique sense of greater purpose, and to pursue your daily quest for human dignity no matter how badly others are behaving."

When I first began my career as a psychologist, it was considered a bit strange and awkward to explore spiritual questions and concerns with a counseling client. But many years of research have shown that if you respect each person's unique spiritual path (and listen carefully to his or her daily concerns about how to live with meaning, purpose, and dignity), a tremendous amount of psychological and physical healing takes place.

Please note that you don't have to agree with every single one of the spiritual, psychological, or neuroscientific ideas we will explore as I describe these eight remedies. One of the things I love about the healing methods of Jewish spirituality is that many of the greatest scholars and rabbis say with humility, "We don't insist on one rigid way of believing. There are mysteries about life, healing, and the Eternal One that we humans simply can't figure out with our limited words or our short-sighted human concepts. So we are always open to questions and respectful disagreements."[2] In fact, several Jewish teachings say that if someone comes along and insists, "I know the one and only answer about what God is like, or what causes suffering, or why a distressing situation is happening to a loved one," you should politely walk away from this dogmatic individual because he or she is probably a fake.[3]

Living with a humble and awe-inspired appreciation of the mysteries that are beyond our shortsighted human capacity for explanation means that there is plenty of room for all sorts of individual interpretations and differing beliefs. In Jewish spirituality, you're encouraged to express your skepticism, to ask lots of questions, and to wrestle intelligently with these mysterious issues. Even the name of the Jewish people—Yisrael (*Yisra,* "to wrestle or strive with," and *El,* the "mysterious Eternal One")—means that like Jacob in the Bible (whose name becomes Yisrael after he wrestles with a dreamlike being in the desert), you are encouraged to grapple with the ever-flowing Creative Source that is beyond human concepts.

So please don't be afraid to debate or respectfully disagree with anything I discuss in this book. In the very act of wrestling—by engaging in these important questions with your entire mind and unique personal experiences—is where you can find genuine strength and deeper insights.

THE REMEDIES

You may be surprised to discover that you don't need to master all eight of the meditation and refocusing techniques presented here to see huge benefits in your daily life and personal vitality. In fact, you might choose to read and experiment with only four or five of these remedies over the next few weeks or months. Or you might focus on just one or two at first, because there are so many other things going on in your life right now.

Briefly summarized, the eight chapters that follow will give you a deeper understanding and specific guidelines regarding any or all of the following:

1. When you're feeling fragmented or pulled in two directions at the same time, the reenergizing "Hineini. Here I am" method will help you feel far more alive and focused.

2. When you are impatient with yourself or others for what is not perfect, practicing the Radical Amazement method will help you outsmart your problem-obsessed brain so you can notice and feel renewed by the many blessings, solutions, and positive supports that you would otherwise miss.

3. When you are too busy to listen to what your body requires to stay healthy, you will get tremendous benefit from taking a quick, mindful moment each morning to say a prayer of gratitude and clarify what is working and what is not on a physical level for boosting your overall health, your digestion, and your ability to deal with the stresses placed on you. Using this daily moment of meditation can significantly change the way you appreciate and respond to your body's crucial needs and vulnerabilities.

4. When it's hard for you to delegate or find others to help lighten your load, the profound *tzimtzum* ("pulling back" or "making a space to empower others") method will give you creative ways to make sure you don't use precious time and energy on doing too much. That way you have extra energy for those situations where you want to be more fully present and highly effective.

5. When there are one or more highly draining people or situations in your life, you will benefit from a wonderful method from the Pirke Avot (*Sayings of the Ancestors*) that teaches how to be strong, compassionate, and wise, even when you are dealing with a person or a situation that is harsh, abrasive, or irritating.

6. If you have recently been hit by a loss, setback, or trauma, I hope you will find inspiration in a fascinating approach to dealing more creatively with such situations. It's called "Gam zu l'tovah. Even this could possibly be for good," and it can help you to honor the genuine sadness and frustration and then gradually open up to the possibility of some hidden wisdom or positive opportunities that might eventually emerge during the healing process.

7. When you momentarily lose sight of your inner strength or higher purpose, a beautiful meditation on the pure soul can be transformative. This method can quickly help you boost your

inner resilience and strength, which you might otherwise fail to connect with on overstressed days.

8. Whenever you feel stuck in a rut or tired of the same old challenges, you will enjoy a rich teaching and daily centering technique called the Shehecheyanu (which means seeing the newness and greater possibilities in each unique moment). It will help you and your loved ones discover a daily state of curiosity, renewed passion, and positive energy, even when you face recurring tension-filled challenges.

My goal in presenting these eight remedies is not to overload you even further or to impose a bunch of additional "shoulds" on you. Rather, I hope that you will choose to approach this book and its teachings as an enjoyable activity and experiment with these holy techniques in a life-affirming way.

Possibly because I'm the child of a Holocaust survivor, I've always been fascinated at how Dr. Viktor Frankl and many other Jewish teachers, health professionals, and creative individuals have been able to use Jewish spiritual techniques to find purpose, dignity, and special moments of joy even during the toughest times. I've discovered that if you study Jewish spirituality (both the ancient and modern teachings) deeply, you will find that most of the spiritual practices are primarily about finding the joy, the healing, and the repair that are possible in life, even when you are facing enormous challenges.

I hope this book will spark happiness, strength, and goodness within you and anyone with whom you share it. These eight focusing methods have certainly been a source of great benefit and healing for me and for many of my clients and loved ones. Every day of my life, I am grateful that someone shared these helpful tools with me precisely when I needed to learn them.

I

A Recentering Method for Any Stressful Moment

IN THE FIELD OF LINGUISTICS, there is a heated debate about icy snow. I'm not kidding. Several linguistic scholars have argued about exactly how many words and phrases the Inuit people who live near the Arctic Circle have developed for the cold, white, frozen particles that surround them every day. Some experts insist that the Inuit language has seven or fewer words for snow, while others say these Arctic individuals have twelve or more slightly different words for the omnipresent icy crystals.[1]

Unlike this scholarly debate, there is absolutely no question about how much most of us in major metropolitan areas currently use a wide variety of words and phrases to describe the element that is omnipresent in our own twenty-first-century lives: stress, the recurring sense of time pressure and tension that most of us experience every day. If you think about it, you will find that the vast majority of human beings in cities and suburbs have developed a fascinating assortment of colorful phrases to describe their inner state on a challenging day, when it feels as if they are being pulled by several competing roles, responsibilities, and pressures at once. Which of the following descriptions sound like you or someone you live with or work with?

- He can barely find time to breathe.

- She's definitely overextended.

- He's swamped.

- She's had an extremely full plate lately.

- He's carrying too much on his shoulders.

- She's up to her eyeballs with this.

- He's running on fumes.

- She's drowning in details.

- He's dying to have some time for himself.

- She's afraid that if she takes a moment to rest, the whole house of cards will come tumbling down.

As a resourceful person, what can you do to regain your strong center and clarity of mind when life feels stressful, when you have suffered a painful setback, or when your to-do list is packed too full? Is there a quick and powerful solution that doesn't require seven days on the beaches of Hawaii or a Caribbean island, that can renew your energy where you are right now in a matter of a few seconds or minutes?

Almost twenty-five years ago, I attended an unforgettable workshop with a wise and humble rabbi named Theodore Falcon, who asked us to spend a few minutes meditating on two short phrases that come from the holy writings shared by Jews, Christians, Muslims, and many others. We were instructed to ask ourselves silently the open-ended question that is asked a number of times in the book of Genesis and the book of Exodus: "Where are you?" We were to do this several times a day, then stop and dig deep to answer it honestly each time.

Stop for a moment, and try this out for yourself. If a compassionate teacher or a still, small voice inside you (one of the names in Jewish spirituality for the Creative Source or the Shechinah, which means the in-dwelling aspect of the Divine) or an ever-flowing Creative Source that you can connect with at certain transformative moments were to ask "Where are you?" silently and supportively, what would be your honest response?

SEVERAL WAYS TO ANSWER

If you sensed this deep and loving question in the back of your mind, you might give a variety of responses. You might describe to yourself where you are spatially—the physical place where you are right now and how this specific place looks, sounds, feels, smells, or has a particular meaning for you.

Or you might answer the "Where are you" question by noticing your breath. Is there some pressure or stress that is causing your breathing to be shallow, uneven, or constricted? Are there some current thoughts and feelings that are causing you to feel rushed, anxious, discouraged, agitated, or unfocused?

You might answer by exploring where you are at this moment in your life's journey: where have you been, and where do you seem to be going? Like waking up from a foggy, fragmented state and suddenly seeing a glimpse of the big picture, the expansive "Where are you?" question can be extremely clarifying.

Finally, you might answer by sarcastically evading the question and replying, "What's it to you?" or "Leave me alone," or "I'm not paying attention right now, because I'm distracted or I'm hiding." (In the book of Genesis, Adam hears a silent and invisible Voice asking, "Where are you?" and Adam admits, "I heard the sound of You. But I was afraid and I hid."[2]) Clearly, we human beings have free will, so we always have a choice of whether or not to respond to the soul-stirring question of "Where are you?"

Now, rather than hiding or being too busy or too distracted, a more effective way of responding to this probing, silent question is to open up your heart and become more fully alive with your answer. There are numerous places in the Torah (the Hebrew scriptures) where a still, small voice or a divine Creative Source calls someone by name or asks, "Where are you?" The response that several of the complicated, vulnerable human beings in Genesis, Exodus, Samuel, Isaiah, and other books of the Hebrew Bible give is a clear, passionate, and mindful reply:

Hineini. Here I am.

Hineini is pronounced "he-neh-nee," and this three-syllable Hebrew word is one of the most interesting spiritual tools I've ever encountered. When you respond to life's challenges, to God, or to your inner turmoil by saying, "Hineini. Here I am," something positive stirs up inside you. Some specific parts of your brain, your body, and your soul come alive and feel energized with new clarity from announcing these words silently to yourself. I don't claim that they are magic words, but quite often I have seen the phrase "Hineini. Here I am" help people in ways that are hard to explain.

Next, we will explore a few of the real-life contexts and profound results that many different people have experienced as a result of experimenting with "Hineini. Here I am." But first I will point out that if you want to learn more about what this phrase means on a deeper level, there is a fascinating recent book that explores each of the times that a silent but deeply moving Voice asks "Where are you" (or calls someone's name repeatedly to get their attention) and the vulnerable individual (Abraham, Jacob, Moses, and others) responds with "Hineini. Here I am."[3]

An easy-to-read book about the Hebrew word "Hineini" was compiled by Dr. Norman Cohen, a brilliant rabbi and Torah scholar who was one of the participants on the PBS series with Bill Moyers about how to interpret the Bible in modern ways. In the first half of the book, Cohen writes about the various biblical examples of responding mindfully to fourteen different "Hineini. Here I am" moments. Then in the second half of the book, Cohen asked eleven male and female rabbis and scholars to discuss their own "Hineini. Here I am" moments when they personally used this centering phrase in order to become more resilient, more fully present, and more open to living with greater purpose and meaning.

PUTTING THIS INTO PRACTICE

Let's take a moment, try these brief but profound phrases silently, and see what they feel like to you. Begin by imagining a compassionate, silent Voice of infinite wisdom or a big-picture Source of Creativity asking you personally, "Where are you?" To do this effectively, be sure to breathe slowly in and out as you hear the silent "Where are you?" Then take just a few seconds to connect with your deepest truth and answer honestly where you are at that moment (physically, emotionally, spiritually, energetically). Please note that you don't need to compose a whole autobiography or long self-analysis here. Just a quick check-in with your best inner wisdom or your big-picture awareness that allows you to state honestly, "This is where I am right now at this particular moment."

Next, with the intention of opening up your heart, mind, and spirit, take another deep breath in and out as you answer silently with a declaration of your willingness to learn and grow, "Hineini. Here I am." Rather than hiding or running away from the urgency of the current moment, let these words wake up your soul, your creative energy, and your inner strength.

As you practice saying the words to yourself, see if your mind and body become a little more focused and stronger each time you say them. Many of my counseling clients tell me their brain seems to become more alert and their eyes can see more clearly when they say these particular words. Others tell me they feel they have opened up a passageway to their deepest inner knowing, and they are able to break free of the surface noises and stresses of the day by doing this energy-boosting exercise. Still others say they feel as if they have taken a dose of truth serum that allows them to sort out what is vital and honest from what is confusing and distracting. What's most important is that you notice whether your ability to deal effectively with the pressure of the present moment is improved by your silent declaration of "Hineini. Here I am."

AN EXAMPLE OF USING THIS QUICK METHOD ON A BUSY DAY

One of my counseling clients, an extremely creative and intelligent woman named Rachel, told me during our initial session, "I have so many things I want to do in my life, but there's this feeling of being overwhelmed and fragmented that I fall into sometimes because I'm simply doing too much. I often have so many stressful things on my to-do list each day that I can't seem to focus sufficiently on just one thing. So I tend to jump from one apparent crisis to another, and I lose perspective on what I really want to be doing." Rachel described how this feeling of fragmentation was causing problems in her career, in her personal relationships, and especially in her health by increasing her craving for carbs and sweets (which often left her feeling sluggish, foggy, and self-critical a few minutes after the rush of pleasure she got from ingesting a sizable dose of delicious treats she knew were a numbing escape).

If I were a traditional Freudian therapist, I might have explored with Rachel what feelings of guilt and parental memories in her unconscious were causing this fogginess or feeling of fragmentation. But since Rachel had already done many years of traditional analysis with another therapist, she specifically wanted to explore some helpful here-and-now tools for dealing more effectively with her high-pressure life and daily stresses: "I don't want to sign up for several more years on the couch. If it's possible, I definitely want some practical methods I can call to mind and use exactly when I'm starting to feel stressed or overloaded."

So I asked her if she would feel comfortable trying a daily centering method that is a bit spiritual in origin. I explained that we would know in a few days or weeks if this method could successfully override her habitual tendencies to feel overwhelmed and to numb out with carbs or sweets on stressful days.

Rachel smiled and said, "I have no problem with something that is a bit spiritual, so long as it doesn't require me to bow down to some guru or start signing up devotees for someone's hokey spiritual agenda."

I appreciated Rachel's honesty and promised that her spiritual life would be entirely up to her, with no guilt or lingering obligations from me. As I do with all my counseling clients, I promised I would not weigh in on what she should believe or not believe; I would merely offer her a few methods that were likely to improve her health and daily effectiveness.

Then I told her about the ancient and modern versions of the mysterious, silent question "Where are you?" and the individual choice of whether or not to respond with a heartfelt "Hineini. Here I am." I asked Rachel to practice it a few times in my office and then to try out it the next several times she was in a stressful or fragmenting situation.

Over the following weeks, Rachel experimented with this mindfulness method in several different settings. One morning when she was stuck in horrendous traffic on the way to an important meeting, she took a moment to breathe, relax, and ask herself lovingly, "Where are you?" For a few seconds, she gently soothed her blood pressure and refocused her mind by noticing where she was spatially, that she was part of a colorful sea of cars and faces— some of the people were tense and angry, while others were calmer, listening to music or enjoying random thoughts.

No longer resisting or resenting her current situation, Rachel was then able to breathe calmly, even though she was still held up in traffic. Then she breathed again and said the words, "Hineini. Here I am." Suddenly she felt strong and reenergized for the upcoming meeting rather than fragmented or drained by the traffic delay. As a result, once Rachel arrived at the meeting, she was far more creative and effective than she would have been if she had burned out her adrenal system in traffic. Like many of my counseling clients who have used this method, Rachel had silently renewed her clarity and strength while dealing with a stressful situation.

Rachel also used the "Where are you?" question and the "Hineini. Here I am" recentering method with her anxious mom. Over the past several years, a phone call or visit with her guilt-inducing mother could often cause Rachel to feel frustrated or fragmented for hours afterward. But when her mom called one busy morning with a series of invasive questions and subtle criticisms, Rachel was able to breathe calmly and say gently and lovingly to herself, "Where are you?" For a few seconds, she comforted herself silently by saying, "I'm having a one-sided phone call with my anxious mother whom I love a lot and who is quite agitated sometimes." Then Rachel breathed calmly again and said to herself, "Hineini. Here I am." She quickly discovered she felt far more alive and stronger, despite her mother's abrasive and intense energy.

As Rachel told me the following week in my office, "That was the first time I can remember that I got off the phone after a stressful phone call from my mother and still felt relaxed and solid. I was able to help my mother with a few of her concerns and still have lots of good energy for the rest of my own busy day."

WHY DO THESE WORDS WORK SO WELL?

There are at least two different ways of explaining what goes on when you stop, breathe, and say, "Where are you?" and "Hineini. Here I am" in the middle of a stressful day. The first explanation comes from Jewish spirituality. The second comes from the neuroscience of the human brain.

From a spiritual perspective, we are more than just material beings having stressful days, because we are essentially spiritual energy forms or souls living on earth within a limited human body. In the Jewish tradition, each person has a pure soul, and each day is a chance to connect or align that pure soul with its Ultimate Source, the hard-to-describe Soul of the Universe.

Like a solar panel that draws strength when it is exposed to the sun, or like an ocean tide that is pulled strongly by the gravity of the moon, our individual souls draw strength from aligning more closely with the nameless and hard-to-explain Creative Flow of the Universe, which Jews call HaShem (the Name that is beyond human knowing), Yud-Hei-Vov-Hei (the breathy and undefined name for God), or Shechinah (the in-dwelling Presence of the Infinite One).

Whatever you choose to call this ultimate source of energy/flow/insight, your daily opportunity is to remember to connect more closely with it and to let it strengthen your inner wisdom and your ability to do good in the world. From a spiritual perspective, the words "Where are you?" and "Hineini. Here I am" can help you, during a stressful moment, to realign with the invisible energy grid that we frequently fail to realize is right there beside or inside us. When you breathe calmly and open your heart and mind to a wisdom that is beyond your five senses, you are reconnecting your precious soul (small *s*) with the infinite Creative Source or the universal Soul (capital *S*).

There is also a scientific, more observable explanation of the same phenomenon. Specifically, we now know from brain imaging research studies that huge numbers of different nerve connections in the brain are dormant or inactive under certain conditions, yet they become active (and light up) under certain other conditions. For example, studies have shown that some parts of the human brain are reptilian (focusing on temperature regulation, basic survival reflexes, food urges, water needs, and sexual desires); others are mammalian (focusing on affection, tactile exploration and grooming, tribal safety and security issues, group cohesiveness, belonging, and kinship rituals); and still others are exclusively human (focusing on concerns such as certain kinds of cognitive problem solving, advanced planning, and loyalty to ideas and identities).[4]

In addition, several recent research papers and books have shown that a series of nerve connections in the human brain light up in brain imaging studies as a result of spiritual moments (such as feeling connected to a higher purpose, a higher power, or a sense of awe toward the wonders of life). Numerous scientists have been able to show that when these spiritual moments occur, portions of the brain are activated because people are seeing the big picture, feeling connected to something beyond the self, or feeling more aligned with the great unfolding of life.

For example, in 2007, Mario Beauregard, a neuroscientist at the University of Montreal, demonstrated how specific areas of the brain can be shown to activate during contemplative prayer and meditation and that when a person goes inside to connect with a Divine Presence, the affected areas are quite different from those activated by hallucinations, autosuggestion, or states of intense emotional arousal. Beauregard and his team found that these brain area activations closely resemble how the human brain processes real experiences rather than imaginary ones.[5]

At the University of Pennsylvania, Dr. Andrew Newberg has been exploring for several years whether the human brain is hardwired for spiritual activity. He's found repeatedly that several sections of the brain are activated in consistent patterns only when the subject engages in nonmaterial, spiritual thoughts and experiences (which cause visceral, measurable neurological events in the brain and body). In other words, according to Newberg's studies, we humans have been given brain capacities and nerve connections that are specifically meant for spiritual thoughts and activities, but they wait for us to activate them before they light up and begin to function.[6]

At UCLA, Dr. Daniel Siegel has written several books on the neuroscience of prayer, meditation, and spiritual experiences in which he's shown how the practice of meditation and mindful states (which he defines as "simultaneous curiosity, openness, acceptance, and love") can definitely cause detectable physical changes in the brain and improve well-being. His research studies at the University of California–Los Angeles have demonstrated that the curious, open human being who learns how to go into spiritual or mindful states of consciousness does something that improves clarity, focus, and health; the brain images for people in such states are clearly distinguishable from those of people who are in a trance or are having hallucinations or fantasies.[7]

So from a neuroscientific perspective, when you breathe calmly and connect with an indescribable Source of wisdom or support by hearing the question "Where are you?" and responding with "Hineini. Here I am," you are essentially activating crucial parts of your brain that tend to be dormant or sluggish at other times. In other words, even if you can't prove the existence (or nonexistence) of a Divine Source, you still have the ability to activate the spiritual, big-picture, and mindful parts of your brain if you choose to do so.

MAKING THE CHOICE TO SHOW UP
MORE FULLY EACH DAY

Regardless of whether you say, "Hineini. Here I am," as a way of answering God's still, small voice or simply as a way to activate a greater portion of your brain's capacity, each day of your life will present you with crucial opportunities for choosing either to show up more fully or to run away and hide.

My favorite "run away and hide" story is the book of Jonah, which many congregations read on the afternoon of Yom Kippur (which can be described as either the Day of Atonement or the Day of At-one-ment). As a young child, I didn't understand or appreciate the Jonah story. It seemed like a bizarre, fanciful tale of a stubborn man who was swallowed by a big fish. But as an adult, I've become fascinated by the realistic depiction of human psychological evasiveness and reluctance that is found in the story. Jonah is a highly intuitive and intelligent individual who hears an intense inner call to go to a place called Nineveh (a large Assyrian city on the Tigris River) to confront the hypocrisy and selfishness there. But instead of doing what the concerned Voice of Wisdom is telling him, he does the two things that most of us tend to do when we are reluctant to show up for what life has in store for us. Jonah runs away (to another town called Tarshish, which is near the Mediterranean in southern Turkey) and falls asleep.[8]

Once you see the story of Jonah as a beautiful description of how hard it is to be fully present or to follow through on what you know inside is the right thing to do, the story becomes a useful reminder that each day we must choose: we can zone out and run away, hoping no one will know, or we can follow through on the tough challenges that life gives us for some inexplicable reason.

For the rest of today and the rest of your life, I can guarantee there will be stressful moments and situations where you may feel overloaded or pulled in several directions at once. But rather than numbing out or running away, you now have a tool you can use to rise to each occasion and be more fully courageous and effective.

As we end this first chapter, here are just a few situations in which you might find it helpful to use the spiritual tool of stopping, breathing calmly, and hearing the silent supportive question "Where are you?" Then when you're ready, you can answer from your heart and soul, "Hineini. Here I am." See which of the following tend to occur for you or for someone you care about:

- When you are sitting in front of a beloved family member, friend, or colleague who needs your full attention and open heart, but your thoughts are starting to drift and your energy is dwindling, take a quick moment to silently ask yourself, "Where are you," and respond with an energizing but silent "Hineini. Here I am."

- When you are stressed and tired from doing too much, but there is something you still need to do with clarity and mindfulness, remember to breathe calmly and say from your heart, "Hineini. Here I am."

- When you think you're in the wrong place doing something that is not as important as what you wish you were doing, it is an excellent moment to stop, breathe, and consider "Where are you?" Quite possibly, you are in exactly the right place for what you need to learn or experience, so it would be important to say silently with passion and curiosity, "Hineini. Here I am."

- When you have been giving a lot to others, and it's time to take a moment for your own needs and feelings, you can stop, breathe calmly, center, and unwind by saying, "Where are you?" and "Hineini. Here I am."

- When things are going well and you've been too busy to take it in or appreciate it, be sure to take a moment to stop and clarify by asking, "Where are you?" and then to become more fully present in this glorious moment by saying, "Hineini. Here I am."

- When you feel alone, unsupported, or off track and you want to reconnect with your inner wisdom or the nourishing creative flow of the universe, take a few moments to ask, "Where are you?" and affirm with dignity, "Hineini. Here I am."

- When you feel frustrated that your busy day is overloaded or stressful and you're not able to be fully present or focused, take a deep breath in and out as you clarify where you are. Then a few moments later, take another deep breath in and out as you switch on the strongest and wisest parts of your essence by saying silently, "Hineini. Here I am!"

2

Outsmarting the Anxious, Moody Brain

YOU MAY HAVE ALREADY NOTICED that there's something problematic about the human brain. Specifically, scientific studies have shown that our brains have an exhausting tendency to focus constantly on things that are unfinished, while at the same time, we tend to overlook or take for granted things that are solid. Left to its own devices, the human brain will almost always find something about which to worry and feel insecure—even when numerous things are going well. No wonder we feel stressed and overloaded much of the time; our brains are primarily focused on the things that are most distressing.

This frustrating habit of the brain to focus on the negative and overlook the positive was first discovered by a researcher named Bluma Gertstein Zeigarnik at the University of Berlin in 1927.[1] A Jewish woman born in Lithuania, Zeigarnik was very interested in how the brain decides what to focus on and what to ignore, so she asked a large number of research participants to look at several types of incomplete pictures and sentences. She discovered that when the human eye looks at a circle that is seven-eighths complete, the brain will usually obsess on the eighth that is incomplete. Zeigarnik also found that when asked to look at a group of random sentences, most people forget the majority of coherent sentences, but their brains stay stuck on trying to figure out the sentences that have a missing word or an incomplete thought. As a result of these studies, nearly every Psych 101 student today learns to memorize something called the Zeigarnik effect—that human beings habitually focus on what's incomplete or negative and that it takes a conscious effort to override the brain's natural, problem-obsessed tendencies so we can begin to notice or appreciate what's positive or going well.

To understand how the Zeigarnik effect impacts your own life, here's a quick example. If you've ever taken a quiz in school, a licensing exam for your profession, or a driver's test for which you have to wait a few minutes, hours, or days for the results, you may have noticed that immediately following the test, your brain and nervous system feel agitated because you're still trying to solve the one or two items that were especially confusing or hard to answer.

You may have forgotten most of the easy questions on the test, but the one or two most frustrating ones may disturb your peace of mind afterward. When you do get the test results and find out that you passed easily, you may still feel a bit insecure, because the one or two toughest questions continue to cause you to worry about your competence or whether you are truly "good enough." For some people, the insecure feeling of "I wonder if anyone will ever find out that I have serious gaps in my knowledge" can last a long time.

So if you have ever felt unresolved or insecure about anything that eventually turned out better than expected, all I can say is, welcome to the human race. We have been given a wonderful tool—a brain that vigilantly seeks out problems and irritations that need fixing. But as human beings, we may not find it easy to trust our brain to notice many moments of satisfaction, joy, or sufficiency. Brain research studies show that to feel incomplete, dissatisfied, or never quite good enough is automatic to most of us because of the way the brain tends to focus on imperfections. On the other hand, to have a sense of "Wow, I'm truly grateful and satisfied in this moment" goes against our brain's basic default software program.

My goal in telling you this is not to depress you, but rather to empower you. Most people trust their own biased version of reality far too much, when in fact the human brain is like a problem-seeking missile that goes out of its way to pay attention to worries, anxieties, and disappointments that are even remotely possible. The brain is an excellent device for finding what could be wrong and then feeling a bit agitated because something is not in its proper place. But that same brain cannot easily notice or recall positive things or good outcomes from even a few minutes ago unless we come up with conscious and deliberate ways to override its unbalanced first reactions.

Let me give you another quick example of why we need an alternative method to outsmart the problem-seeking, moody brain. In a relationship with a spouse, lover, partner, or roommate, your brain will naturally tend to ignore or forget the hundred kind or helpful things the other person has done. But your brain (like every other human brain—I hope you won't take this as criticism because we're all in this together) will, more often than not, focus on the two or three things he or she does that irritate or worry you.[2] As a result, on a busy stressful day when you're tired or drained, you're likely to snap at the essentially good and caring people closest to you, as if they can do nothing right. How often do you find yourself irritated with a loved one or coworker who is 95 percent wonderful and only 5 percent clumsy or imperfect?

Does this seem reasonable—to be on the edge of snapping at people you care about because your brain is only able to concentrate on what they've done wrong? Does it seem fair to ignore all the things they've done with kindness and to lash out angrily (or secretly harbor a long-festering grievance) because of the two or three inconsiderate or frustrating things they've done? How can we build a positive relationship with someone who's human and imperfect when we each have this slightly unbalanced thinking device in our head that focuses heavily on what's incomplete or irritating?

Even the most well-educated and intelligent of us tend to ignore or take for granted the positive, considerate things others have done for us. Is it possible to feel relaxed, healthy, or somewhat secure on a daily basis when our brains are constantly looking for trouble?

HOW JEWISH SPIRITUALITY OUTSMARTS THE ANXIOUS, STRESSED BRAIN

Many centuries ago (before there was scientific proof), certain rabbis and teachers explored the limitations of the human brain and whether people could connect with a joyful, expansive level of reality that went beyond their mind's anxious, dissatisfied first reaction to daily events. These ideas and suggestions are at least two thousand years old (some scholars say twenty-four hundred[3]), and there are indications that they were spoken by the leaders of the Great Assembly in Jerusalem more than two millennia ago, when the sacred Temple was still standing.

What the rabbis and teachers recommended then (and it remains true today) was that people should outsmart their worried, dissatisfied brain by reconnecting frequently with a sense of awe and appreciation for the many gifts and wonders that their anxious mind tended to forget or overlook. To avoid being bogged down in fears, insecurities, and feelings of sluggishness, the spiritual teachers came up with daily blessings that people could say when they faced difficulties or felt uncertain about the future. These scholars (who had stressful lives of their own) designed a series of specific, short phrases to overcome the heaviness and moodiness of the human brain and allow the soul and inner energies to rise to higher levels each time the words were said.

Instead of letting yourself become chronically stressed, burned out, or exhausted by the pressures and responsibilities of your daily life, you can renew your soul and your body at crucial moments during a busy morning, afternoon, or evening with this Jewish practice of saying a sincere, heartfelt word of appreciation. Rather than dismissing what's going right in your life (and only noticing what's going wrong or what's incomplete), you essentially send your nerves, muscles, and arteries a healthy dose of joy and vitality each time you stop for a quick moment to notice something wonderful or awesome as you offer up thanks to the Ultimate Source of that wonder and awe. Or in the words of the twentieth-century Jewish scholar and teacher Rabbi Abraham Joshua Heschel (who marched with Martin Luther King, Jr., and wrote several highly regarded books on how to live each day with greater purpose and joy), you begin to practice "Radical Amazement."[4]

According to Heschel, Radical Amazement happens when you become more open to the many exquisite moments and cherished insights in a busy life that previously seemed to comprise too much rushing and too much pressure. He urges us to rise consciously above the stresses of modern life for brief moments numerous times a day throughout the week and to become more aware of all the awesome mysteries and wonders we usually race past without fully noticing.

If you want to experience a glimpse of how to live each day more awake, alive, and healthy, you can begin right now by experimenting with a highly effective method for overriding the constant problem-seeking tendencies of your brain. There is a remarkable blessing phrase that seems to encompass all the other blessings. Many times in my own life (and in those of individuals with whom I've shared it), it has transformed anxiety or stress into a renewed sense of mindfulness, strength, and happiness. This 2,400-year-old blessing consists of six profound Hebrew words that I will translate and explore with you so you can decide which meanings and interpretations feel most empowering for your daily life.

The words are as follows:

Baruch (Blessed is)
She-amar (the One that constantly speaks or expresses or creates)
V'hayah (and it comes to be)
Haolam (the world around us and inside us)
Baruch hu (Blessed is He/It/this awe-inspiring Process).

If you say it together as one easy-to-remember phrase, you have:

Baruch she-amar v'hayah haolam, Baruch hu. Blessed is the
One that is constantly expressing and the world comes to be.
Blessed is this awe-inspiring Process.

You will notice that the six Hebrew words don't try to define
what God is or isn't. They simply alert us to the fact that there is
some Creative Source, which in this particular blessing is called
"the One that is constantly expressing." And this Creative Source—
whatever you call it—is continually infusing the energy flow that
keeps the world around us and inside us alive.

In Judaism, there are many ways to imagine the One that is
constantly expressing and creating. Please don't think that you
need to settle on a particular limiting image of God that some
insistent teacher or family member has told you must be "the only
one." In fact, in Judaism, there is a strong emphasis on humbly
admitting that any image or concept of God you might be temped
to think is "the entire answer" is probably far less accurate than
what the Eternal Creative Source truly is.

PUTTING THIS INTO PRACTICE

This six-word blessing has been recited throughout the world
many millions of times—during traditional Jewish morning
prayer rituals and as part of Sabbath morning prayers. It also can

be said in your own daily life whenever you see something beautiful, something alive, something mysterious, something good, something curious, or someone about whom you care deeply. Each time you say the blessing (in Hebrew or English or both), you are telling your body and mind, "Take a moment to fully breathe in something wonderful and true."

I admit I didn't grow up saying this particular blessing very effectively when I was a child in Detroit. Like most people, I raced through it when I would attend a Sabbath or weekday morning service. Not until I was an adult studying Jewish meditation did I find out that these six profound words hold a remarkable power that causes your brain to stop obsessing about what is incomplete or frustrating, so that you can experience a moment of joy and satisfaction at what is right in front of you.

As a result, I frequently take a moment to say these six words slowly and carefully whenever I first open the drapes and look out at the trees, birds, flowering plants, and human activity in front of my home. Or I say them whenever I see a person doing something interesting or compassionate. Or before I sit down for a conversation with my wife or son. Or whenever I see some aspect of nature that is beautiful or awesome. Or whenever I see something creative or original or heartfelt happening.

I find that these words, both in Hebrew and in English, can turn a moment of anxiety or frustration into a surprisingly transformative opportunity for deep gratitude, curiosity, and vitality. Instead of becoming burned out or run down, I feel alive and renewed each time I say this blessing slowly and consciously with a deep breath.

A FEW ALTERNATIVE WAYS OF SAYING THIS BLESSING

Some people I've counseled aren't comfortable with Hebrew words or religious prayers and blessings; they simply say, "Wow! That's amazing," when they sense something beautiful, creative, or compassionate happening around them. Others who are more traditional and at ease with religious blessings tend to say, "Baruch HaShem (Blessed is the Name of the Eternal One that is beyond any name or human concept)" at these moments. Others simply say, "Thank you, God," "Here's something I'm grateful for," or "Let me breathe for a moment and appreciate that."

Still others who favor a feminist approach to spirituality use the Hebrew words, "B'rucha Yah (Blessed is the Breath of Life that is blessing us right now)." Or they say, "Blessed is Shechinah (the in-dwelling Presence of the Eternal One) that surrounds us and gifts us with so many blessings." Finally, some people find it difficult to remember the six-word Hebrew phrase, so they shorten it to "Baruch She-amar (Blessed is the One that is constantly expressing)." Or they say a blessing using their own spontaneous, original wording; for instance, saying silently or out loud to a friend or loved one, "Something happened today that I don't want to overlook. It made me feel good that _____ happened."

If you have been reluctant to say prayers or blessings in your own informal way, please note that it's absolutely permitted to do so. According to the well-known Orthodox rabbi, physicist, and scholar Aryeh Kaplan, author of the fascinating book *Jewish Meditation: A Practical Guide,* "There seems to be a feeling that Jewish prayer must be in Hebrew, in a prescribed manner, with a predetermined wording. Many Jews were surprised to learn that there is an unbroken tradition of spontaneous prayer in the Jewish religion. Rabbi Nachman of Bratslav, the brilliant and revered great-grandson of the founder of the Hasidic tradition, the Baal Shem Tov, taught that the most effective method to attain a strong personal relationship with God is personal prayer in one's own native language."[5]

Regardless of what words you use (Hebrew, English, or the language you grew up with), Jewish spirituality recommends saying a blessing and stirring up a positive flow within your body and mind numerous times each day. Even on a busy day, many teachers and scholars say we can definitely aim for at least a hundred quick moments when we consciously take note of something large or small that is beautiful, awesome, or beloved and then spontaneously say a quick blessing to wake ourselves up to the amazing world that the Infinite Source has created.[6] Some recommend thirty-six blessings a day.[7] Others say to start slowly with two or maybe five times a day. However many times you choose, you can begin to override your problem-seeking brain and notice something positive as you say, "Baruch HaShem, Blessed is the Name of the One who creates," or "Baruch She-amar v'hayah haolam, Baruch hu. Blessed is the One that is constantly expressing and the world comes to be, Blessed is this awe-inspiring Process" to yourself. You can also achieve this when you say to a family member or friend, "Something that inspired me recently was when _____."

For a moment, be honest with yourself: exactly how many times today have you been willing to break free of your brain's anxious thoughts to notice something large or small in your life for which you feel grateful? During the stressful and busy moments of the past several hours, have you been able to fully appreciate any blessings or things that are going right?

If you are like most people who have complicated and intense lives, your answer to the question "Got gratitude?" is probably a sarcastic "Yeah right, in your dreams," "I'm too busy for that," or "Maybe later, after I finish what's on my to-do list."

Let's face it, most of us are constantly swept up in the problem-seeking dictatorship of our brain. We are essentially enslaved by what it has told us is more important than breathing itself. To free your stressed body and mind from this chronic *mitzrayim* (a Hebrew word referring to the enslavements of ancient Egypt and translated as "constriction," "a narrow place," "limited thinking," or "suffering") you might begin by experimenting with the uplifting, mind-shifting technique of saying several sincere blessings a day. Then notice if these moments of mindfulness and appreciation improve how you deal with the many stresses of daily living.

THE MAN WHO RECEIVED A HUGE DOSE
OF ANXIOUS GENES

My friend and colleague Richard is a good example of how some-one used the phrase "Baruch She-amar, Blessed is the One that is constantly expressing" to great effect. Richard is a hard-working computer consultant who grew up in a family of extremely high-strung individuals. According to him, "In my family tree, there are a bunch of very anxious and, to some extent, obsessive folks who became successful in fields where precision and careful plan-ning are crucial skills. I wouldn't call us fun-loving or easygoing, but in terms of receiving a huge dose of anxious, anticipatory, highly intelligent genes, we did quite well."

This genetic gift of a strong, vigilant brain and the ability to anticipate problems was a huge career advantage for Richard and each of his family members. For example, his dad was an engineer who worked on the Mars Rover projects. In the field of engineer-ing, it's important to have a highly cautious brain that can seek out and address what might go wrong. For an engineer on a multimil-lion-dollar project, it pays to be especially vigilant and cautious about preventing costly mistakes. In fact, many experts have said that if someone at NASA had been more obsessive and worried ahead of time about what might happen to an O-ring on the Chal-lenger space shuttle if the outside temperature was unusually cold on the morning of the launch in January 1986, then the famous school teacher Christa McAuliffe and the entire crew might still be alive today.[8]

But as Richard explained to me one afternoon at lunch, "In my work as a computer consultant, it's great to have a brain that can anticipate and address every possible difficulty. Yet in my mar-riage and my relationships with my two kids, that kind of anx-ious, problem-focused brain can be abrasive and irritating—or so I've been told."

Specifically, Richard found that his strong attention to detail and his ability to find fault (in order to be proactive and anticipate solutions) caused his wife to consider him "a chronic micromanager who's always accusing me of not doing enough to keep order in our home." His two children were frustrated that he was constantly finding fault with their schoolwork, their friendships, their appearance, and their career dreams. As Richard's eldest daughter told me, "My father has this impatient look on his face almost every night and every weekend that says, 'You're not living up to my expectations.' It's exhausting to be his kid."

Like most men, Richard had been unwilling to go to individual therapy, and he'd been fairly uncooperative when his wife dragged him to a few extremely unproductive couples counseling and family therapy sessions. As he told me, "Everyone wants me to change, but this happens to be who I am. I'll admit that I have high standards and I just can't hide it or fake it when I'm feeling let down or disappointed. I'm hoping my family will realize that I criticize them because I love them and want the best for them."

Does Richard's story sound like yours or that of someone in your life who is a highly intelligent professional? Are the precise standards and vigilance that make you successful at work getting on your loved ones' nerves? Are there times when the problem-focused brain that is so helpful in some areas of your life causes pain for and distance from the people you love?

Since we've known each other for years and often give each other honest feedback, I asked Richard if he would be interested in trying something unusual to lighten up a bit toward his loved ones and make his life a little more enjoyable and healthy. He looked a bit hesitant at first, but he became a little more interested when I suggested, "It's just an experiment to find out what it would feel like to be 40 percent less anxious."

He agreed to "experiment" for a few weeks with the daily practice of noticing positive things and saying a silent blessing with sincerity to see if it would cause a noticeable drop in his overall feelings of anxiety. He was willing to focus his brain for a few weeks, not just on problems and things that might go wrong, but also on things that went right and a few awesome moments when his five senses noticed something beautiful or satisfying.

A month later we had lunch again, and Richard described what had transpired since our previous conversation: "I was doubtful during the first several days that saying some Hebrew and English phrases was going to make any kind of a dent in my lifelong tendency to be a basically anxious and unhappy person. But despite my skepticism, I was walking down the street one evening after a long day of working with clueless, frustrating people on their computer problems, and I smelled a whiff of night-blooming jasmine. Normally I would be completely inside my head, focused on some frustrating moment of the day or some computer glitch that I needed to figure out for the next day. Only because I promised to try out this experiment for a few weeks did I stop for a moment and say a blessing that some remarkable chain of events had put this amazing fragrance in my path at the end of a stressful day. And for just a few seconds, I felt a little bit freer and more alive than I usually do. Since that time, I've upped the number of blessings each day from two to almost twenty. My wife and my kids tell me I'm becoming less irritating at home. They actually saw me smile a few times, and they were shocked that I was patient and forgiving once or twice when there was a lot of disorder in the living room."

Richard began to notice over a period of several weeks that he was gradually retraining his brain to not just find fault but also to be persistently aware of things for which he was grateful. According to him, "I've still got a strong and effective anticipatory brain that can be proactive at resolving problems that others fail to see. But as a result of this daily experiment of noticing what's going right, I see a lot of things now that I previously overlooked. It's as though I used to have black-and-white tunnel vision, and now I've added a much wider range of colors and insights to my visual field. Recently each night my family starts dinner with a new ritual— either Three Things That Went Well Today or Three Things for

Which I'm Grateful. By the time each person has spoken, we feel a lot more connected and a lot less defensive and antagonistic."

WHAT MAKES THIS DAILY PRACTICE SO SUCCESSFUL?

There are at least two possible explanations of why the actual process of saying these daily blessings with sincerity can cause your mind and body to be less anxious and stressed. I invite you to consider whether one or both of these perspectives seem reasonable to you.

The first comes from Jewish spirituality. When you open your heart and your energy several times a day to notice and acknowledge a large or small blessing, you are essentially participating more actively in the *Shefa* of the universe. *Shefa* is a Hebrew word from the mystical or Kabbalistic tradition that can be translated as "flow," "ever-flowing Divine energy," or "how the Divine transmission enters the physical world."[9]

To understand the importance of Shefa or the process of flow in the universe, we need to talk about the word *God* for a moment. Like most people, you may have grown up thinking that *God* refers to a father figure in heaven who looks like the white-bearded old man in the Michelangelo paintings. But in Jewish spirituality, especially in the mystical tradition of Kabbalah, the Divine energies are more like a rainbow of light shining on us or arising from within us, or they comprise a fountain of blessings that is constantly flowing. The popular image from European art of a white-bearded old man is far too anthropomorphic and limiting, while the metaphor of a fountain of blessings transmitting light and wisdom constantly into our human existence (if we are willing to open up to it) is offered by numerous Kabbalistic writers.

The metaphor of the Divine Shefa as an ever-flowing abundant energy has been discussed more extensively during recent decades. In fact, during the 1990s, an acclaimed Jewish feminist scholar and writer named Marcia Falk wrote a widely praised book of

prayers and meditations in which she consciously avoided the typ-
ical metaphors of God as a father figure. She focused instead on
how to connect with a more mystical and Kabbalistic type of God,
an invisible Source of abundant loving-kindness and compassionate guidance, an ever-flowing Fountain of Blessings.[10] I first met
Marcia at a conference in 1984, and I have been inspired by her
writings and teachings ever since. Her ability to inspire thinking
about God and the ultimate life force in new (and old) ways has
been helpful to many people throughout the world.

So if you envision the Source of Life as an ever-flowing, abundant fountain, then from a spiritual perspective, when you say two
or thirty-six or a hundred blessings a day, you are consciously
aligning yourself with the many large or small blessings that are
all around and inside you (if only you remember to notice). You
are opening your heart and mind to a flow of healing energy that
has enormous power to inspire and renew.

From a scientific perspective, the daily practice of noticing and
commenting on the large and small blessings of your life is a way
to stimulate and increase the flow of neurotransmitters in your
brain, cells, and nerve endings. As you probably know, there are a
few specific feel-good chemicals (such as serotonin, norepinephrine, and dopamine) that lubricate the crucial connections between the nerves and cells in the body. Thousands of research
studies have shown that you tend to feel good and alert when you
have the right amount of these important neurotransmitters or
lubricators flowing through your cells (either because you have recently done a lot of exercise, taken a vigorous walk, had an or-
gasm, or engaged in a pleasurable conversation or creative activity,
or because you took a prescribed medication that caused your
brain cells to hold on to your serotonin and other neurotransmitters longer than usual).[11]

On the other hand, when you are tired, stressed, depressed, or
highly anxious, your neurotransmitters or cellular lubricators tend
to get depleted. You might also be among the many millions of

people whose serotonin, norepinephrine, or dopamine gets biochemically washed out of your system every so often, even when external events aren't especially stressful. When you're running low on these key neurotransmitters, you tend to feel edgy, impatient, or volatile—as though your nerve endings are metal rubbing against metal without sufficient lubrication.

According to science, saying numerous blessings each day (and noticing what's going well in your world) can boost your internal supply of nerve-cell-lubricating neurotransmitters. Stopping for a quick moment several times a day to say a heartfelt thank-you to the fascinating chain of sources for the blessings around you stirs up additional feel-good chemicals in your brain and nerve endings. In essence, you are manually giving yourself the right levels of serotonin, norepinephrine, and dopamine that your body and mind require to function at peak effectiveness. Rather than letting your problem-obsessed brain ignore what's going right (and thereby deplete your energy reserves), you take back your power and remind your brain that it's time to boost the neurotransmitters that are crucial to overcoming worry, anxiety, depression, and stress-related sluggishness.

FINDING YOUR OWN UNIQUE WAY OF SAYING THANK YOU

I mentioned earlier that in Jewish spirituality it's permitted and encouraged to offer prayers, blessings, and expressions of gratitude in your own words. To speak from your heart and to be honest as you share your joys, pain, confusion, or lingering concerns with the silent Source that can be found deep within your soul is extremely appropriate. In fact, the first example of someone praying in the Bible is Hannah (in the first book of Samuel), whose lips moved as she poured out her sadness and frustration at being childless and her deep desire to become pregnant. Some onlookers thought she was strange or mentally unbalanced because her lips were moving, but in fact she was the first healthy role model for how to use honest, spontaneous words to express our longings and how to share those words from the heart with the Ultimate Source of all that exists.[12]

When Hannah did become pregnant, she said thank you by naming her child Samuel (which is Hebrew for "God has heard"). Unlike most of us, she didn't ignore her good fortune or take it for granted. Each time she called her son by name, she reconnected with the joy of knowing that there was an abundant Source that had given her a beloved child.

While I cannot guarantee that every prayer or blessing you utter will lead to the precise result you want, I can definitely say that speaking honestly, one-on-one, with the Ultimate Source of creation and flow (whatever you believe that Source to be) can resonate in your body as a deeply uplifting experience. Connecting in your own words with the ever-flowing Soul of the Universe (especially with gratitude for large or small blessings) is often an effective way of putting yourself back together when the stresses and frustrations of your life make you feel fragmented or off track.

For the rest of today and the rest of your life, you can experiment with saying thank you to the Fountain of Blessings that is constantly expressing within and around you. If there is someone in your life whose love or support means a lot to you, take a moment to thank in your own words the Creative Source that breathed life into that individual. If your body, mind, or spirit is thriving, talented, compassionate, wise, or helpful and you want to boost your energy as a result of these gifts, then make sure to say a blessing or a thank-you to the One who helped you become this way. Or if there is a moment when your senses notice that something in your world is beautiful, nourishing, inspiring, or unique, let yourself be reenergized by saying words of this blessing.

Even if you are currently saying a grand total of zero blessings or just one thank-you each day, see what happens to your clarity and your moods when you start focusing your mind on the many things in your life that are going well and shouldn't be taken for granted. You will probably find that your nerves, heart, breathing, and thoughts become a little less stressed each time you outsmart your anxious brain by manually boosting your cell-lubricating neurotransmitters with a sincere blessing of thanks.

3

Becoming Healthier So You Can Deal with Stressful Days

ON AN OVERFILLED DAY, when you're rushing from one obligation to the next, does your body ever say silently, "Hey, what about me? Why am I being ignored again?"

Most people say they care about their health and longevity. But how do you find sufficient time to take good care of your fragile body when there is so much else to do and so many other things to handle in your life? That's the dilemma I've discussed with thousands of therapy clients. I've found that the vast majority of people with busy or stressful lives have usually discovered a few reasonable strategies over the years for improving their weight, nutrition, physical vitality, stamina, resilience, and daily self-care. But they often get thrown off track by extremely full schedules or unexpected demands on their time; then their well-intentioned health goals and positive routines are put on hold.

For example, do you (or does someone else you care about) have some specific health goals and positive self-care routines that seemed doable when you first attempted them but ended up being hard to maintain? During a hectic day or an exhausting week, do you ever find that your best strategies for dealing with food, exercise, and stress management get tossed aside? Do you often sense that you are falling into old, numbing habits or that you are unable to get back to your positive health routines once you've slipped a bit?

For many people, there's a vicious cycle regarding health and vitality. On a stressful day, your body definitely needs extra care. Yet there's usually not enough time or energy, so you try to ignore your body's needs instead. As a result, the feeling of being overloaded increases, and your body becomes even more sluggish or compromised.

A RADICALLY DIFFERENT APPROACH

In Jewish spirituality, there's a highly effective, short meditation phrase about health and how the body works. I've found it extremely useful in my own life and with many of my counseling clients.

This easily understood phrase has quite a long history of helping people get a clearer sense of their own health challenges and their best strategies for improving their physical well-being and longevity. In fact, in the Hebrew Talmud (which consists of numerous commentaries and conversations on how to live a sacred life), there is a vivid description of a highly pragmatic and inspiring series of words that can be recited daily to increase your awareness of the wonders of your body and the definite possibility of boosting your physical health.[1] This ancient blessing draws from specific Biblical verses (Exodus 15:26 and Judges 13:19), and you can find it in most Sabbath and daily prayer books in any synagogue, bookstore, Jewish library, or home.

Unfortunately, most people in the twenty-first century have never been taught this useful prayer, or if they have been told to recite it daily as an obligatory ritual, they usually say it quickly, without much awareness of what it really means. When I've given workshops for various congregations and adult education programs across the United States, I've been amazed at how many people who do know this phrase say it without much *kavanah* (the deeper intention and sincerity that can make a specific prayer, meditation, or ritual far more meaningful and helpful).[2]

When I think of the word *kavanah,* I remember back to when I was a teenager attempting to pray at my grandfather's traditional synagogue in Detroit. Many of the people in the congregation seemed to be racing through the prayers so quickly that they didn't find much connection to what they were saying. So I asked my grandfather, "Why don't people slow down and really take what the words are saying to heart?" My beloved grandpa looked at me with a smile on his face and replied, "If you want to go slow and really connect with what the words are saying, go ahead. No one will get upset or ask you to leave."

Please take a moment to consider what your experience with prayer or saying various blessings has been. Is it about rushing through the words to fulfill an obligation, or is it about opening your heart and connecting with the deeper meaning? Several key Jewish writings say, "God doesn't want your sacrifices or your empty rituals, but God wants your open heart."[3] It's crucial to find the kavanah, or deeper intention, that connects you with the truth of what you are saying.

So maybe it's time for a reexamination and a rediscovery of this short phrase about keeping your physical body healthy and flowing. In the spiritual toolbox of Judaism, this particular blessing consists of a few profound ideas that may surprise you with their bluntness and graphic content. In its full, three-sentence version, this blessing/meditation describes the sense of curiosity and awe you would feel if you were to stop for a moment and genuinely consider how miraculous it is that the human body works as well as it does. To understand what these three sentences mean for you or your loved ones on a personal level, imagine for a few seconds what would happen if your lungs, nasal passages, throat, or mouth were blocked and you couldn't breathe. Or if the valves of your heart weren't working and you couldn't pump blood and oxygen throughout your body. Or if there were an obstruction somewhere in your vast digestive system with its valves, nutrition-sorting absorption cells, waste-discarding organs, and twisting intestinal tunnels. Or if there were a blockage in one of the many blood vessels or nerve connections of your brain that prevented oxygen and blood from flowing smoothly to the cerebral cortex so you couldn't think clearly, move gracefully, or balance yourself, or communicate effectively?

What would happen to you if just one of these crucial parts of your vulnerable physical apparatus were substantially compromised? On the other hand, consider for a few seconds just how many thousands of things function well at the present moment in your body and mind so that you are able to connect coherently with the words and ideas found on the page in front of you. Think about what an amazingly complicated and intricate gift your physical body is.

Here are the actual words you can say daily with sincere understanding, humility, and appreciation:

Blessed are You, Eternal Source of Creation, Ruling Force of the universe, who has fashioned the human being with wisdom and created within each person many openings and many cavities. It is obvious and known before Your Throne of Glory that if but one of them were ruptured or but one of them were to be blocked, it would be impossible to survive and to stand before You. Blessed are You, O Eternal Source of Creation, who heals all flesh and acts wondrously.

It is traditional to say these words right after you go to the bathroom. Or you can say them during a moment of morning prayer or centering before you start your busy day. I find it fascinating that in Jewish spirituality even the most private moment of releasing the toxins from yesterday's food is treated with mindfulness, appreciation, and deep compassion for the delicate and brilliantly constructed body we have been asked to care for by the hard-to-define Creative Source that infused us with so much life force energy.

Notice that this three-sentence meditation explores a few worst-case scenarios that could happen ("if but one of these openings were ruptured or blocked") as well as the fact that a miracle truly happens each day ("Who has fashioned the human being with wisdom . . . many openings and cavities . . . to survive and stand before You"). This daily moment of insight can help you remember all day to balance the joy of eating with a careful awareness that your body needs the right ingredients, fibers, fluids, exercise, and vitamins to function and keep you alert and alive.

FINDING YOUR OWN SPONTANEOUS WORDS

Many people say a shorter version of this blessing to stir up their own sense of gratitude, healing, and physical vitality each day. There are several possibilities, and I hope you will choose the full or abbreviated version that feels most honest for your situation.

Those who are unsure about believing in God tend to shorten the meditation/blessing by saying, "I am so thankful for being alive and being able to stand here with my body working as well as it does," or "Wow, this body is an amazing gift, and I better not take it for granted."

For those who have a glimmer of faith or a moderately strong belief in a Creative Source called God or Infinite One, a shorter version of the meditation is to say, "Thank You, Creative Source, for putting wisdom into my body so that it can absorb so much nutrition and then release what is so toxic," or "Thank You, Infinite One, for all the many things that are working well enough right now so that I can stand before You and express my appreciation at what You have given me."

If you have a deep and intimate relationship with a Divine Presence that you call God, Shechinah (the in-dwelling Presence of the Divine), or HaShem (the Name of the One that is beyond human description), then you are asked to take a moment and say with sincerity, "Thank You, thank You, thank You, Infinite Source of Life. I am so aware right now that You have given me the precious gift of life and a body that needs great care. Ribono shel Olam (Master of the Universe), You amaze me, and I am so glad to be able to stand in Your Presence and thank You for one more day of enjoying a healthy flow that allows me to live with purpose and compassion."

Regardless of what you believe or don't believe, you can take a moment to find your own unique words that express exactly your awareness of how easy it would be for your body not to be working and how profound it is that your well-designed but sometimes fragile body is doing specific, crucial things each day to stay alive. Quite often the most effective prayers, meditations, and blessings are those that come spontaneously from the heart at the moment you notice what a wonder it is to be alive and functioning so miraculously.

In addition to words spoken in their own language, many people find that the original, holy Hebrew words have an additional power to bring healing and strength. These 2,000-year-old words can be said by anyone with deep sincere emotion and awareness:

Baruch Atah, Adonai Eloheinu, Melech haolam, asher yatzar et haadam b'chochmah, uvara vo n'kavim, n'kavim, chalulim, chalulim. Galui v'yadua lifnei chisei ch'vodecha she-im yipatei-ach echad meihem, o yisateim echad meihem, i efshar l'hitkayeim v'laamod l'fanecha. Baruch Atah, Adonai rofei chol basar umafli laasot.

Now, please reread the full English translation silently or out loud one more time with new eyes and ears. What do these words say to you now about your relationship to your physical body and your awareness of the precious gift of life you have been given? Once more, recited with a deeper understanding than the first time you said it, this prayer can be translated into English as:

Blessed are You, Eternal Source of Creation, Ruling Force of
the universe, who has fashioned the human being with wisdom and created within each person many openings and
many cavities. It is obvious and known before Your Throne
of Glory that if but one of them were ruptured or but one of
them were to be blocked, it would be impossible to survive
and to stand before You. Blessed are You, O Eternal Source
of Creation, who heals all flesh and acts wondrously.

PUTTING THIS INTO PRACTICE

If you want this remedy to significantly benefit your health and
vitality each time you say it, I recommend a crucial follow-through
step that has made an enormous difference for many who have
tried it. Right after you say the full Hebrew or English prayer (or
a shorter, spontaneous version in your own words), take a moment
to ask yourself some honest questions about what you are willing
to do, starting right now, to keep up your end of the partnership
that exists between yourself and the Creative Source or life force
that gave you this fragile and wondrous body.

What does it mean to you to be a crucial partner in taking the
necessary actions to help your body become healthier and more
vibrant? Usually when children or passive adults pray for healing,
they tend to ask God or some all-powerful Other to do all the
work. Yet the important follow-through step requires something
different, something more interactive and decisive. The majority
of Jewish scholars, rabbis, and teachers have said for many centuries that simply praying passively for health and healing is not
enough. In Judaism, human beings are considered to be God's
agents or God's language for bringing about positive results on
this earthly plane of existence.

For example, the daily self-care you do, the doctors and health
advisors you pick, the persistence with which you act on current

research findings about how to stay vibrant and energized—these are the ways you perform what Hillel (a great teacher in the first century before the Common Era) described as "the sacred duty of taking care of the body, the home of the soul, that is created in the likeness of God."[4]Maimonides, the twelfth-century scholar, writer, physician, and community leader, described it as, "To walk in the ways of God, it is a person's duty to avoid whatever is injurious to the body and then to cultivate habits conducive to health and vigor."[4]

In Jewish spirituality, it's not a matter of just offering a one-directional plea to heaven for healing; rather, it is making sure you live up to your mutual partnership with the essential life force that brought you to this dance called life. If you want to be a more effective partner for the necessary improvement of your health and vitality, then each day after you go to the bathroom, or as part of your daily meditation practice, it is essential to say the words of gratitude and also to use this meditation as a moment of truth seeking—asking yourself exactly how well you are taking care of the delicate physical apparatus that has been given to you.

During this private moment of profound honesty, you can quickly explore each of the following questions:

- What exactly did I eat, drink, or do yesterday that made my body work well today (or not work very well today)?

- What seems to cause my body and mind to get sluggish, foggy, blocked, or agitated?

- What specific steps am I willing to take today so that my body gets the amount of nutrition, water, fiber, exercise, stretching, relaxation, sleep, expert advice, and safe medicinal support it needs to function better?

- What exact changes or improvements do I need to establish today so my body and mind will thrive and heal?

- If I truly believe that God or life has given me this extremely precious and fragile gift of a complicated body that has hundreds of openings, valves, and organs that can easily be ruptured or made ill, what am I willing to do—starting today—to be a better guardian or caretaker of this gift?

THE WOMAN WHO MANAGES MUSICAL DIVAS

What do you predict might happen if you were to start using the ancient meditation and truth-seeking questions I have described? I often find that intelligent and dynamic men and women (who have started to neglect their health somewhat because of their stressful daily schedule) are able to make tremendous progress in taking care of their bodies in a few days or weeks—even if they have had setbacks with various weight plans, fitness center regimens, or health strategies that they weren't able to follow consistently in the past.

For example, Caryn is a music industry executive who made an appointment for counseling because of her stress headaches, her digestive complaints, and her sleep problems. Her physician had put her through a variety of tests and concluded that she needed to do something about her severe stress levels. In counseling, we did some excellent work on how to deal more effectively with her explosive boss and her self-absorbed music industry clients (to whom she referred as "my exhausting divas"). But to fully resolve her physical symptoms, Caryn needed something more.

So I explored with her the possibility of using the daily meditation for health and the truth-seeking questions that go with it. Caryn told me that even though she was "not a very religious person but somewhat spiritual," she was willing to experiment with this meditation method for a few weeks to see if it produced beneficial results. Despite the fact that she was busy launching a worldwide tour for one of the musical groups she manages, she set aside a few moments each morning for her quick meditation about health. After a few weeks of using the three-sentence blessing, she saw her role as the caretaker of her fragile body in a new light. As she discovered, "I'd never really sat down and asked my body what it needs and what seems to cause sluggishness or agitation."

Over the next several months, Caryn began to eat in a less rushed fashion, and she was far more motivated to avoid the foods and habits that might disrupt her sleep or jeopardize her overall health and alertness. She explained, "This daily moment of thinking about what my body requires and what it can't handle has helped me to start treating my physical self as a gift that deserves special care. With each day of doing this quick check-in technique, I've begun to see a number of positive results, especially the fact that I started drinking more water throughout the day and exercising more to keep things flowing. I also decided to do fifteen minutes of enjoyable walks at least five times a week and fifteen minutes of stretching in my bedroom each morning."

During her tenth and final counseling session, she admitted, "It's quite bizarre. If someone had said to me six months ago that I would be losing weight, feeling stronger, and having much better digestion because of a morning prayer or meditation technique, I would have dialed 911 and had them come and take this loony person away. But to my surprise, this quick moment of spiritual connection and gentle truth seeking each day has kept me on track week after week. I'm no longer bingeing and dieting with all sorts of inconsistent results. It's more of a loving moment of opening up to a truthfulness and an infinite Wisdom that can help me take good care of my delicate body one day at a time."

THE MAN WHO COULD NO LONGER JOG

Here's one more quick example about how to use this daily meditation successfully, even if there are serious obstacles in your stressful life that have recently made it difficult for you to take care of yourself. It's the brief story of a man named Dennis, whose family tree has a significant genetic predisposition for depression, heart disease, and strokes.

Dennis described to me how his father suffered from depression and several of his relatives had been hospitalized for heart problems. Yet for many years, he had kept himself fit and energetic by jogging each day.

Unfortunately, a few months before he initially came in for therapy, Dennis had severely injured his knee. As a result of the intermittent pain in the tendons and ligaments surrounding the joint, he stopped exercising and began to put on weight. He also started to experience a frequent sense of impatience and irritability, an unhealthy rise in his cholesterol level, and a noticeable increase in depressive thoughts.

As Dennis told me during his first counseling session, "You don't have to sell me on the importance of healthy diet and daily exercise. I've been a jogger for years. But what am I supposed to do now? I can't run any longer because of my knee. I might have to go for surgery eventually, yet for now I'm just stuck in a daily rut of not getting the blood flowing. As a result, I've become a lot less creative and a lot more moody."

Does this sound like you or someone you know? Did you at one time have a healthy way of increasing your vitality and positive moods? Have you, recently or over time, lost the ability or the willingness to take proactive steps to take excellent care of your body? As a result, are you starting to notice a decline in your physical energy and an increase in your edginess or your internal agitation?

To help Dennis get back in shape, we first did some counseling work to explore his frustrations at "no longer being able to trust my own body." I asked Dennis if he'd be willing to try something unusual and somewhat spiritual that might or might not help to get his positive energy back. He was hesitant at first about trying anything spiritual: "I grew up in a religiously rigid home, and the last thing I want to do now is put my faith in something that reminds me of what my parents and my older brother used to force me to do."

After hearing a few examples about his painful experiences with several dogmatic "Do as I say or else" relatives, I decided to respect his wishes and began to offer him other types of relaxation methods from the field of mind-body psychology. But then Dennis interrupted me and said, "Wait a minute. Even though I don't like the harsh, inflexible beliefs I grew up with in my family, I'm still open to the possibility that there's some unexplainable energy we can tap into. I'm wondering if this spiritual technique that you wanted me to try might work even if I have a lot of doubts and skepticism."

I told Dennis about how this particular meditation or blessing had shown excellent results with the vast majority of men and women who'd tried it, whether or not they considered themselves religious, spiritual, or somewhat uncertain. He looked at me carefully and then said, "As long as no one tells me what I have to believe or tries to turn me into a zealot or a fanatic, I'd be willing to give it a try."

I asked him if he wanted more time to think it over, but he insisted, "Let's go for it."

During the next two counseling sessions, I explained to Dennis how to use the three-sentence blessing for health and the daily self-care, truth-seeking questions. Over the next few weeks, he tried it out each morning at home. At his fifth counseling session, he told me, "It's strange about this ancient prayer I'd never heard of before. By saying it each morning, I've gotten far more motivated about improving my health, even if I have an injured knee. And I find myself wanting to try new things besides jogging or running, which I always assumed was the only way for me to stay in shape."

One morning while he was saying the health meditation silently and asking himself the follow-through questions, he got a new idea. He decided to call and ask his old friend from high school who was now a physical therapist how people in wheelchairs or with hip and knee problems get their daily dose of aerobic, heart-pumping, mood-lifting exercises. His friend recommended a fifteen-minute series of customized exercises that can be done using an eight-ounce plastic water bottle as a prop. The therapist also suggested a few DVDs, available online and in many music and bookstores, on how to do chair aerobics and stretching exercises.[5]

I recommend that you be careful and consult with a trusted doctor, physical therapist, yoga teacher, or knowledgeable exercise instructor on how to do these daily stretching and aerobic techniques safely.

The carefully designed exercises from the physical therapist and from two of the recommended DVDs were extremely beneficial for Dennis. Not only did he enjoy the fifteen minutes of daily aerobics that he achieved, but he also noticed that his depression lifted somewhat, and he had far more patience for dealing with stressful situations at work and with his family. According to Dennis, "I'm still a little frustrated that I can't jog anymore, but I love the fact that these chair and floor aerobics have made me healthy and fully alive again."

WHY DOES THIS DAILY PRAYER WORK SO EFFECTIVELY?

From a purely scientific perspective, the daily blessing is so effective after going to the bathroom because it clarifies in your mind the twenty-four-hour physical cycle of how toxins get released and the body stays healthy. If you take just a minute each morning to ask yourself honestly, "What did I do in the past twenty-four hours that made things flow smoothly (or not) in my body this morning," you will discover important truths about what kind of diet, exercise, and relaxation your body is receiving or needs.

In essence, this health-awareness blessing helps you become a far more honest and savvy guardian of the particular body and digestive system for which you are responsible on a daily basis. You are taking a moment each morning to do a daily behavioral self-management inventory that you can refine and improve whenever you want to achieve even better results. From a spiritual perspective, the daily health prayer and the truth-seeking questions can give you the strength and momentum to overcome the numbing-out impulse with which we all grapple on a daily basis. (Honestly, it's not just you. We each struggle daily to avoid things that can jeopardize our health.)

In Jewish spirituality, every human being has a *yetzer tov* and a *yetzer ha'ra*. The word *yetzer* means a creative energy or urge that can be used for either good (*tov*) or harm (*ha'ra*). Every day of your life you will have moments when you feel pulled by your yetzer ha'ra, the escapist, numbing, or sneaky urge that causes you to do things that are physically gratifying for a few seconds but are not life-sustaining in the long run.[6]

Quite often the seductive pull of the yetzer ha'ra, the inclination to indulge in what is momentarily delicious and somewhat self-defeating, is extremely compelling and persistent. In fact, the relentless urge to your mind and body to indulge in instant gratification tends to be far more compelling and hard to resist than the still, small voice of the yetzer tov, the creative urge to do what your big-picture self knows is best. In Jewish spirituality, one of the ways to strengthen your good inclination (yetzer tov) is to surround yourself daily with pleasurable reminders and supportive tools for doing what is healing and nourishing for the long run.

On a stressful day when you are battling an urge to eat something unhealthy that will taste wonderful for a few seconds but will later plug up your digestive system or leave you feeling bloated, foggy, or sluggish, you are up against your yetzer ha'ra.

Or when you can't seem to get yourself to do the physical exercises or follow the balanced, healthy lifestyle choices that you know intellectually your body needs, then you are probably being coaxed or pressured by a sneaky or destructive urge: "Forget about exercise or taking a walk right now. Just eat a few delicious cookies and grab the remote control. No one will know."

In Judaism, you're not considered a bad or hopeless person if you are tested daily by your yetzer ha'ra (your agitated or numbing energies).[7] When you are tempted to do something harmful to yourself or others, that is a holy moment when you have an opportunity to remember that you are essentially a pure soul with a higher purpose. These are the moments when saying a blessing or taking a quick moment for silent meditation or prayer can turn your creative thoughts in a positive direction.

Rather than bombarding yourself with guilt or self-loathing, it helps to quickly and lovingly raise your awareness as to your true essence and mission in life. From that higher perspective, you can then find the strength and focus to be able to say no to the urge to do something harmful and say yes to the urge to do something positive or good. From a place of compassion for your delicate body and gratitude for the gift of being alive, you will probably feel better able to choose something life-sustaining and healthy as your next meal or activity.

It's not easy much of the time. The yetzer ha'ra is cunning, baffling, and persistent. This persistent urge will probably tell you all sorts of lies and half-truths to get you to eat junk food or say no to your plan to exercise or drink more water.

I hope you will be strengthened by this daily moment of truth to seek out how to take better care of the fragile and wondrous body you have been given. Most of all, I hope you will enjoy many years of good health and alertness.

4

Discovering When to Intervene and When to Let Go

ONE OF THE BIGGEST SOURCES of stress and overload that affects us deeply in our lives is when we try to make a positive impact on important situations that are, to some extent, out of our control. For example, have you ever felt drained or frustrated from being thwarted when you tried to influence any of the following:

- A spouse, lover, or roommate who is resistant to being given advice or suggestions?

- A young person in your family or where you work who goes all out not to be controlled by you or anyone else?

- A coworker, client, customer, supplier, or employee who isn't quite reliable but doesn't like being told what to do or how to do it?

- An aging parent or other relative who definitely needs your help but who says frequently, "Let me do it my way."

In addition to the many people you encounter daily who are somewhat resistant or uncooperative, there are also numerous situations in which you can get all knotted up with impatience or frustration because you can't seem to get things to turn out the way you want them to. It might be an irritating call to the phone company, the cable company, or an insurance company where you first have to wait on hold with an automated menu and then you can't seem to get a caring person to help you. Or a malfunctioning computer or other mechanical device that simply won't cooperate despite your best efforts. Or a creative project or home improvement goal that keeps getting delayed or held up by factors you can't control. Or a political, social, or cultural issue that you want to see take a positive direction but that has frequent setbacks and opposition.

I've found as a therapist that the issue is not just that someone or something is resisting your efforts. On a deeper emotional level, it often feels as though you are powerless or invisible when you find that your strongly held values and goals are being ignored or defeated. We human beings enjoy having a sense of mastery, competence, or forward momentum. So it can be frustrating and draining when, on a stressful day, you have one, two, or several incidents in which you try to do something helpful or constructive, but instead repeatedly feel thwarted.

THAT ELUSIVE THING WE CALL CONTROL

Since we have gone through several chapters together, I hope it's okay if I ask you a few slightly personal questions. You don't have to say your answers out loud; merely think privately for a moment about your personal frustrations regarding times when you have felt uncomfortably controlled by someone else or when someone has suggested that you (sweet, wonderful you) might be acting a bit too intense or overbearing in a particular situation. Please note that I'm not calling you or anyone else a control freak, but I hope you will briefly consider each of the following stressful situations that bring up the dilemma of how much to intervene and how much to let go:

- Have you ever sensed or been told by someone you care about that you have a tendency to do a lot for others and as a result sometimes (unintentionally) don't make enough room for those individuals to find their own strength or the rhythm to do things their own way?

- Have you ever been told by a loved one, roommate, or co-worker that you are sometimes too overbearing or that you occasionally micromanage something that others would like to handle with less intense involvement and advice from you?

- Have you ever said to a creative partner, child, parent, sibling, or friend, "Why are you constantly going against me on this? I know the right way to do it, if you would just trust me and stop resisting."

- Have you ever wondered, "Why do I give so much to so many people and situations, yet I don't seem to find anyone giving as much to me in return?"

I'm not asking you these questions to criticize you. Frankly, I have struggled with these same issues for many years in my own life (both when I was on the receiving end of someone trying to micromanage a project and when I was told by others that I was being too "hovering" or much too "helpful").

This push and pull between the part of us that wants to be hands-on and in control versus the part of us that knows we ought to kick back somewhat and let others do their fair share is more than just a theoretical inquiry. In fact, as a psychologist, I've found repeatedly that one of the surest ways that good people become severely stressed or burned out (at their job, in family situations, or at life in general) is when they tend to feel out of balance because their urge to arrange or control things is intense compared to their willingness to be receptive or to make room for others to pull their weight in a stressful situation.

Finding an excellent balance between how much to help and how much to step back and make room for others to do more is rarely simple or obvious. For example, several years ago, when my son, Steven, was almost seven and a half, I realized that it might be difficult for him to learn how to ride a two-wheel bicycle. Because of specific physical coordination problems, many of his friends were also having trouble learning how to get rid of training wheels and staying balanced and upright on a "big kid" bike.

I began to hear from several of the other parents at my son's innovative school for creative children with special sensory needs: "We've given up. Our child can do many things well, but he or she is just not going to be able to ride a bike. The physical coordination thing is just not happening."

Watching my son try his best but still fall painfully from each attempt was heartbreaking. If you have ever tried to teach a young child to ride a bike (or if you have watched someone else trying to do it), you probably know the uncertainty of having to decide how much to help (by holding on to the moving two-wheeler while your child pedals intensely) and how much to let go (to allow your child to discover the precise motor memory independently without you holding on).

This delicate issue of how much to intervene and when to let go tends to be hard to navigate in all sorts of real-life situations. Knowing how to make suggestions or offer help to someone without causing a struggle for control is a finely-tuned skill that doesn't come automatically to most of us.

A PROFOUND TOOL FOR DISCOVERING BALANCE

Many years ago, I experienced a wonderful breakthrough on these issues when I learned about a subtle and holy way of balancing how much to get involved and how much to make room for others to come forward. To help you understand this highly useful balancing method from Jewish spirituality, I need to take you on a brief historical detour so you will know the fascinating origins of this insightful perspective which is called *tzimtzum* (pronounced as two syllables, "tzim-tzum").

It's a Hebrew word that means to simultaneously pull back, conceal, or contract your overbearing energy while actively making room for others to be inspired and to bring forward their own spark on how to cocreate that which you are hoping to bring to fruition.[1] In other words, it's about creating something positive, while at the same time pulling back so you don't overpower what you are creating.

In the sixteenth century, in the hillside town of Safed in northern Israel (if you've ever been there you might have noticed that Safed has some of the most inspiring sunsets and enchanting winds of any place on earth), there was a brilliant teacher of Jewish mystical texts and day-by-day spirituality named Rabbi Isaac Luria, who first taught the world about the idea of tzimtzum. His ideas about the origins of the universe and the mysteries of how creation is still unfolding have inspired millions of Jews and non-Jews for more than four hundred years. One of the things I find most fascinating about Luria's teachings is that they were extremely radical and unusual when he described them in a series of carefully transcribed lectures in the 1560s. But in the twenty-first century, his ideas make enormous sense, whether you are a pure scientist, a spiritual mystic, or someone who is open to both points of view.

Luria suggested that the Creative Source of the universe originally transmitted an energy force so intense and vibrant that this infusion of light shattered the finite vessels that weren't strong enough to hold such an overwhelming amount of energy, wisdom, and unfiltered brightness. This theory turned out to be quite similar to the big bang theory that scientists discovered in the twentieth century.[2]

According to Luria, in order to create a livable, sustainable world and to allow humans and other creations to have free will and some independence, this ultimate Creative Source needed to pull back somewhat and conceal Itself in a process called tzim-tzum (which is often translated as "partial contraction"), while at the same time infusing the world with subtler forms of light, wisdom, and an ongoing flow of creative energy.

This tzimtzum idea of concealed invisible energy—which because of its concealment and partial contraction actively makes room for the material world to exist and evolve—had many similar aspects to the theory of invisible dark matter that various scientists discovered in the twentieth century.[3] The widely accepted but still controversial modern theory of dark matter says that our universe consists of a huge amount of energy that cannot be seen or measured directly by humans, but this invisible dark matter is the energy component that continually holds together and subtly impacts the material world that we can see and measure.[4]

I apologize if that was too much science on a busy day. Please don't worry if the big bang theory and the concept of invisible dark matter make your eyelids feel heavy. What is far more important regarding these lofty ideas for our lives is that Isaac Luria gave us a gift that we can use whenever we are beginning to lose the balance between the part of us that wants to control things and the part of us that wants to lighten up and not become frustrated or burned out.

The Secret to Being Creative

Here's how to benefit from this profound spiritual and scientific concept. Imagine what your daily life would be like if you could learn how to emulate or use this idea of tzimtzum (partially contracting, lightening up, making room for others, creating by letting go of control, and bringing out the best in those around you). What if you could gradually discover how to be a more effective vehicle of creative energy in all the important areas of your life, not by controlling things 100 percent, but rather by actively opening up a two-way partnership and inspiring sparks of brilliance and quality to emerge from each living thing around you?

You can understand this two-way, interactive balancing method more clearly if you think of a gardener who learns exactly how much watering and sunlight a plant needs to grow, but who also discovers when to pull back and let the growing process unfold without doing more than the plant can handle (such as overwatering or exposing it to too much sunlight). Or a potter who learns how to gently guide a piece of spinning clay to rise up and become a vase with just the right amount of involvement, at the same time pulling back to allow the form to emerge (and making sure the vase doesn't collapse because he or she pushed against it too hard). Or a teacher, counselor, coach, parent, or mentor who discovers exactly how much inspiring energy and how many helpful ideas to offer, while at the same time pulling back and making room for the unique individual to come to his or her own discoveries and sense of empowerment.

Some people make the mistake of thinking that tzimtzum refers to a complete contraction or an abdication of any involvement. Yet according to most scholars, it does not mean withdrawing completely or shirking your responsibilities. Nor does it mean abstaining from your purpose in life (for instance, seeking to repair your particular corner of this broken world). It means doing your part *and* becoming quiet enough, humble enough, and receptive enough to hear the inner wisdom that guides you on when to let go and stop interfering (so that the person or thing you are trying to help won't be smothered or disempowered and will be able to rise to the occasion).

At the moment when you start to push too hard or get too attached to imposing your will on someone or something, it will be a crucial breakthrough if you can remember to say the following meditation to yourself silently, gently, and calmly:

Tzimtzum. Relax, lighten up, make room, pull back somewhat, and let this process emerge with just the right balance of involvement and receptivity.

Instead of repeatedly getting stressed out when a situation doesn't cooperate with your cherished plans, it's extremely healing to connect silently with the word *tzimtzum*. It can act almost like a gentle mantra or a sensible guiding principle whenever you are trying to create something new or improve something important in your life without becoming overbearing or exhausted from pushing too hard. Just for a moment, practice saying silently, "Tzimtzum. Make room, lighten up, pull back somewhat, be open, become more receptive."

The Moment of Letting Go

When I wanted to help my son succeed at riding a two-wheeler, I found that if I held on too long to the moving bicycle, he kept failing to push hard enough on the pedals; if I gave him too many instructions, he would get exasperated that I was bombarding him with too much parental advice. Yet if I backed off too quickly and let him pedal on his own, he kept falling. Then with his bruised skin and wounded pride, he would say, "I give up. I hate this. I can't do it." There were tears in his eyes, and I began to wonder if we should abandon the bike-riding project and move on to something else.

Then I remembered the spiritual teachings I had learned about the lightening up process of tzimtzum (making space for teamwork and not pushing harder than is warranted). Seeing my son's pain and frustration, I felt a wave of compassion moving up from my heart into my throat. I decided to take a few deep breaths as I silently thought about the meditation: "Tzimtzum. Let go, make room, pull back to allow something creative to emerge." I decided to loosen up the anxious, vigilant sense of control I had been feeling each time we had worked on this bike-riding challenge. Taking one more additional breath in and out, I said silently, "Tzimtzum. Make room for Steven to find his own rhythm and his own sense of balance."

It's hard to describe, but these gentle breaths and the reassuring silent words gave me a new sense of openness and centeredness. With a more soothing and less pressured tone of voice, I was able to say to my son, "I love you, Steven. I love you no matter what happens here today. Let's try it just for the fun of it one more time and see what happens."

I held on to the back of his padded bicycle seat to keep him upright as I ran alongside his intensely pedaling feet just long enough for Steven to get some momentum going. Then I visualized the words, "Tzimtzum. Make room, open up some space," one more time as I let go of the seat. Suddenly my son was riding on his own power. He didn't know at first that I had let go. Probably he was still feeling the love and support between us, along with his belief that I was holding on to make sure he didn't fall.

But to his amazement, he soon discovered he truly was propelling the bicycle's forward motion on his own and was absolutely free of my control. That was the beginning of Steven making enormous progress toward becoming a safe and successful bike rider. It took many more sessions of offering him gentle support and then pulling back to let him discover the motor memory and the habit of riding smoothly without my help or interference. Now it is several years later, and my son loves to go on long bike rides with his friends or with one or both of his parents. What once seemed impossible has become a source of frequent joy and togetherness.

PUTTING THIS INTO PRACTICE

If you like the sound of the word *tzimtzum,* please feel free to use it as a silent balancing device whenever you are leaning too far toward trying to manage a stressful situation that is not 100 percent within your control. Or if you prefer the English words, "Lighten up, pull back, make room, or bring out the best in others," you can use these phrases instead. Or you may benefit from a combination of the mystical Hebrew word *tzimtzum* as well as the more familiar words from your native language that remind you to breathe, open up, be receptive, and actively make room for others to shine.

In my counseling practice, friendships, and volunteer activities, I have seen the tzimtzum meditation method help a wide variety of individuals. More than anything else, the breakthroughs that occur seem to stem from the way the word *tzimtzum* can inspire people to lighten up internally and come across more calmly and lovingly to others.

Instead of overwhelming your own central nervous system with too much adrenaline from vigilantly trying to control things that you mostly can't, the moment of partial pulling back and lightening up allows your body and mind to be a lot less edgy and intense. From a scientific perspective, it's similar to when you sit in front of a biofeedback machine that gradually trains your breathing, glandular system, and heart rate to slow down so you don't pump more adrenaline than necessary.[5] But in a real-life, stressful moment, you can train your body and mind to connect with the release word *tzimtzum,* which will remind your heart, adrenal glands, and racing thoughts to lighten up a bit.

This gentle process of letting go of the need to be controlling and vigilant can then allow you to speak much more gently and encouragingly to the individuals who have been resisting or rebelling against your stressed tone of voice in recent days and months. It also allows you to brainstorm together for creative solutions that your resentment, anxiety, or overbearing energy made unlikely in the past.

For the next few weeks, whenever you sense that you are becoming too attached, too rigid, or too controlling with someone who is habitually uncomfortable with your somewhat exasperated or judgmental tone of voice, please take a moment to breathe in and out as you say to yourself, "Tzimtzum. Make room, lighten up, don't overpower this person."

HOW WELL DO YOU DELEGATE TO OTHERS AND BRING OUT THE BEST IN THEM?

The phrases "letting go," "lightening up," and "empowering others" might sound like attractive ideas. But are you truly ready and willing to surrender some control and let other people have more input into important situations that you formerly handled on your own? Have you sometimes had difficulty delegating tasks to others or getting the cooperation and support you thought you wanted? Do you occasionally worry, "What if when I pull back and trust others to do their fair share, they let me down just like I've been disappointed so many times in the past?" Do you think, "What if I finally open up and ask for help and support, but I'm dealing with people who simply don't care enough to do a high-quality job?"

Please know that you are not alone in having these concerns. The vast majority of busy and highly competent people I've spoken with about these issues admit they've often been frustrated in the past when they've tried to delegate specific activities or ask others to pitch in and help lighten the load. They frequently feel let down when the person to whom they delegated the task didn't seem to care or didn't perform at a sufficient level of quality or commitment. Some of them find it uncomfortable to delegate tasks because they have an underlying feeling (based on previous frustrating experiences) that it's quicker and easier to simply do it themselves in their own way and not be too dependent on someone else.

I wish I could say, "Go ahead and do it all on your own without relying on anyone," but you and I both know that your schedule is already overloaded and that many of your goals and dreams require the support and assistance of numerous individuals.

Since none of us has sufficient time and energy to do everything by ourselves, there's got to be a better way of delegating part of the responsibility and getting much better results than those achieved in the past. There must be a better way to talk about the teamwork you need and find that the other person truly listens and cares enough to do a great job.

Over the past twenty-five years, I've been researching how the tzimtzum method can sometimes change a lifetime tendency of being let down by others. In fact, I've found repeatedly that even a quick tzimtzum moment of mindfulness can significantly improve the probability of a successful outcome from delegating and teamwork conversations between you and the person whose help you definitely need. There are no hundred percent guarantees, but I've found that when you learn how to pull back partially and make room for the creativity and sincere involvement of another person, it works much better than when you treat this individual as someone you need to micromanage or tell what to do all the time.

Here are a few step-by-step guidelines that can help you combine the relaxed mindfulness of the tzimtzum meditation with the nuts-and-bolts specifics of how to delegate far more successfully.

A Step-by-Step Method for When and How to Ask for Help

Step 1. Be willing to try something that is unusual and far more effective than the way people normally interact at work, in families, and in friendships. The first step is to visualize you and the other person helping each other out as allies rather than becoming adversaries. While gently saying to yourself, "Tzimtzum," or "Make room, lighten up," take a moment to breathe in and out calmly several times. Imagine that this time you are going to find a way to communicate your needs more successfully than you've ever done in the past and that you are probably going to be met with more support and teamwork than you've had on previous attempts at delegating to others.

Step 2. Get smart about how to delegate only those tasks that you don't want to do on your own, while holding on to those tasks that can only be done by you (or that you enjoy so much you don't want to give them away). Take a moment—either in your own thoughts or by writing on a piece of paper or a computer—to select two things you strongly want to do in your own style and don't want to delegate to anyone who doesn't share your level of quality or commitment.

Step 3. Pick two things that you are willing to let go of entirely, and allow other individuals to do these particular tasks in their own style and with almost no micromanaging or very little input from you.

Step 4. Finally, pick two shared tasks for which you feel comfortable using someone's best efforts to lighten your load or to showcase his or her talents. Acknowledge that you would like these tasks to be done with specific quality suggestions from you and back-and-forth discussions between you and the other person as equal, collaborative teammates.

You will notice that this step-by-step process of delegation offers a balance between too much control and too little. Based on your sincere preferences, you are given the opportunity to select carefully which things to do on your own, which things to let others do without much input from you, and which things to approach as a shared collaboration between effective partners. Each time you do this step-by-step delegation process, I urge you to select wisely so that you honor your gut feelings and your inner wisdom about how much to be involved and how much to collaborate with another creative soul to be part of the balanced teamwork.

This last step is crucial if you want to safely pull back from doing too much and foster successful teamwork and a satisfying outcome from assigning some parts of projects to people you can trust. For the past twenty-five years, I've been refining this step so that when people who have tended to do too much in the past and get burned out or exhausted take the leap of trusting someone to lighten their load, they won't be let down. It all depends on a few key communication elements that are discussed in the next section. I hope you will read them carefully and try them out whenever you are asking for help or delegating tasks to someone whom you really need to do a good job.

DEVELOPING A MORE EFFECTIVE SENSE OF TEAMWORK

Here are the specific issues that need to be addressed if you are going to create more teamwork and fewer struggles and clashes over control.

Ineffective Ways of Asking for Help

Before we look at what works successfully, it helps to review quickly what doesn't work. Most of us have a few habitual ways of asking for help that are self-defeating and ineffective. See if any of the styles that follow resemble how you or someone you know have asked for help in the past.

The "I Don't Want to Have to Ask" Method. Some of us are a bit uncomfortable about stating exactly what we need (often for fear that we will be disappointed again), so instead we tend to remain silent or say to ourselves, "I'll wait and see if this person cares enough about me to figure out what I need" or "I'm not going to make a fool of myself by asking directly, but I will float a few humorous complaints or subtle hints about what's going on and maybe that will cause this person to find out what's required."

Then when the other person doesn't do what we essentially refused to spell out clearly, we feel upset but secretly vindicated: "See, I knew that no one can be counted on. I knew I'd have to do this by myself eventually."

The "I'm Tired of Being Ignored and Now You're Going to Hear from Me" Method. At the opposite extreme from the silent method, many of us ask for help by waiting until we're burned out, resentful, or frustrated and then blurt out a sarcastic or angry request for help that drips with contempt. For example, have you ever heard yourself or someone else say, "Doesn't anyone around here care enough to lift a finger to help out?" or "What do I have to do to get someone to do their fair share?" or "Why am I always the one who gets stuck doing the lion's share of the work" or "What am I, your servant?"

These exasperation-filled attempts to win someone's cooperation might feel justified because of all the times this person and others have let you down in the past. But these guilt-inducing comments usually don't bring out the best in anyone—they simply cause the other person to roll his or her eyes and say silently, "Oh boy, here we go again with the victim stuff. I'll do as little as possible just to calm things down, but I won't really put my heart and soul into this." Or you might find that your spouse, roommate, child, and/or coworkers simply tune you out when you snap at them. They've learned to protect themselves by keeping their distance from you at times like these and waiting until you take care of things on your own without their help or support.

The "I Need to Spell Out Every Detail Because No One Else Is Reliable" Method. Finally, the third method is the one chosen by most people who tend to do things themselves and are uncomfortable delegating tasks to others. This method is to show up with lists, charts, and carefully designed plans on how you want things done. Maybe you even stayed up late or sacrificed all your free time during the day to come up with these intricate lists of exactly what you want the other person to do.

While the materials may be technically accurate, unfortunately, there's a crucial ingredient missing. Please forgive me for pointing out that you probably skipped the steps of inspiring and empowering the other person and of making room for that person to give his or her best effort. It's one thing to create a step-by-step program for a computer or a cell phone to follow, but human beings require something a little bit different. When you want to collaborate successfully or delegate an important task to someone who will do an excellent job of handling it for you, there needs to be something human and empowering that causes this individual to rise to the occasion.

A More Effective Way of Communicating Your Needs and Preferences

Now we're ready to experiment with something that has repeatedly been shown to be much more successful than any of the previous approaches. If you want to pull back somewhat and free up some of your time and energy for other things on your daily schedule, you will benefit enormously from this easy-to-follow method. I call it the Successful Two-Way Teach Me Conversation. Here's how it works.

Imagine that someone in your life has been underperforming or not doing his or her fair share to make things easier for you on an important project or goal. It might be someone you live with who is refusing to share the load, expecting you to cater to his or her needs. Or it might be someone at work who doesn't seem to care enough to do a high-quality job in a timely fashion. Or someone in your personal life who isn't responding to your requests for teamwork or cooperation. Rather than bombarding this person with criticism, guilt, or vigilant micromanaging that causes him or her to want to rebel, try the idea of tzimtzum instead, and pull back somewhat to make room for the other person to rise to the occasion.

This works best when you take several deep breaths, sit down calmly with the other person for an unrushed conversation, and say with caring and openness some or all of the following (use these words if they feel right to you or change them to your own way of speaking):

Hey, I need your help on something. I need you to teach me how to improve the teamwork between us. I don't want to breathe down your neck or tell you what to do. I definitely respect that you have your own good ideas and your own way of doing things. So let's just take a moment and have you teach me what we can do differently to bring out the best in both of us. Please let me know now or at any future time what feels like the most encouraging and inspiring help we could give each other to keep us both on track as we pursue this goal together as teammates. Please teach me how to be supportive of who you are, and let me know what will help you feel more passionately involved and creative on this particular project.

Or you could use a shorter version:

Hey, I need your input on this. Please teach me what I can do to make room for your ideas and suggestions on how to improve things here. Also, let me know whenever you feel I'm being too controlling, because I want this to be an enjoyable and successful experience for both of us.

Then pull back and listen calmly. Let the other person brainstorm with you in an open conversation, without you immediately criticizing or dismissing his or her ideas. Let the suggestions percolate for a while before the two of you start to edit or refine these ideas to decide together which ones are most likely to be effective. In essence, you are stepping back from the role of boss, critic, parent, rival, overseer, or dominant partner and choosing instead to be a more humble and receptive copartner. Instead of competing over who's right or who's in control, you can use the tzimtzum perspective for making room, and the Two-Way Teach Me Conversation to clarify what feels like teamwork for both of you and what would cause either of you to shut down or tune the other person out.

This method of conversation works especially well when there has traditionally been a power difference or a personality clash between the person who was in the role of overseer and the person who defied or rebelled against the overseer. Here are a few quick examples of how this conversational method can shift a stone-walled situation or a battle of egos into a more satisfying, collaborative team approach between two individuals with equal voting power over the situation.

The Caregiver and the Person in Need. For many years I've counseled a wide variety of caregivers: adults with aging parents, health professionals with rebellious or noncompliant patients, parents with stressed or differently abled children, and others. I've found that when the caregiver jumps in too quickly to do everything for the ailing or stressed person, a sense of resentment, noncooperation, or silent defiance often occurs in which the ailing person feels as if he or she is being treated like a baby and is not willing to give up his or her dignity and whatever sense of independence that still remains.

This power struggle can be alleviated if the caregiver takes a few deep breaths, slows down the adrenaline rush, and silently says, "Tzimtzum. Lighten up, make room for whatever this person can still do without someone else's help or interference."

Then the caregiver can initiate a positive, Two-Way Teach Me Conversation using calming words such as the following:

> Please teach me what I need to know about the tasks you absolutely want to do without anyone else's help, what tasks require just a minimal assist from me or others, and what tasks you want me to take over entirely to free up your energy for other things. Also, please correct me gently when I overstep my role and start doing too much or failing to let you do things your own way. Most of all, tell me whenever you and I get out of balance between times when I want to help you versus times when you want to try something out to see if you can do it without my help.

This kind of conversation will often create a major shift in a stressful situation so the caregiver is no longer overwhelmed from doing too much and the person receiving care finally has a voice to stand up for his or her dignity and independence.

The Busy Parent and the Rebellious Child. Whether you are dealing with a rebellious preschooler, a defiant teenager, or a stubborn young adult, the goal is not to overpower or overwhelm this beloved child with your parental advice or micromanagement. Rather, breakthroughs tend to occur when you remember to pull back a bit at key moments, breathe calmly, and say to yourself, "Tzimtzum. Let me do just enough to keep my child safe but then let go and inspire this growing person to come forward with his or her own way of feeling strong and self-directed."

It works best if you take a few moments once a day or once a week to say to this smart but stubborn young person, "Teach me what I'm doing that feels like I'm treating you as someone who is younger or less capable than you really are. Teach me which things you want me to help you with and when you want me to watch from a distance to let you do things your own way, as long as you are safe." Only if you can get out of the way a little (and stop the power struggle) will your child discover his or her own strength and internal resources.

The Team Leader and the Team Members. At work and in volunteer activities, we often unintentionally exert too much control over someone who needs a little more independence and encouragement to bring out his or her best efforts. That's why it's so important to sit down and have a humble conversation every so often that explores how to encourage collaboration:

Teach me what we could do better, you and I, to bring out the best in both of us. I am relying on you and your smarts to get certain things done. But I don't want to breathe down your neck or tell you exactly what to do, because that would only cause you to feel micromanaged and held back from your own creativity and motivation. So whenever you have some ideas, teach me what I can do to be a resource for your creativity, your solutions, and your best way of dealing with things. And most of all, let me know gently whenever you feel I am hampering your creativity and your enthusiasm because I'm giving you too much input or when you want a different type of input and support than what you've been getting.

Having a mutually respectful, two-way conversation like this doesn't mean you're abdicating your role as the boss, supervisor, or team leader. It simply means you're switching from a patronizing, controlling viewpoint ("I know what's best for both of us, and you're just a pawn in my game") to a more empowering style ("Teach me how to bring out the best in both of us so we can enjoy doing this important project together and rise to a higher level than we have before").

The Motivated Partner and the Hesitant Partner. Let me give you one final illustration of how the tzimtzum perspective can cause a breakthrough in lightening your load and delegating to someone more successfully, even if this person has offered resistance or achieved less-than-ideal results in the past. It's the true story of a couple I counseled. The overworked and frustrated wife, Sandra, was concerned about going out of town to visit her ailing mom. Sandra didn't feel she could trust her husband, Edgar, to be in charge of their two children during her absence.

Like many couples who clash over the issues of sharing child care, domestic chores, and financial stresses, Sandra and Edgar frequently became resentful and frustrated due to increasing disagreements and disappointments in their relationship. They had stopped making love, and their frequent arguments and temper flashes were upsetting to their children and to their own stressed-out central nervous systems.

According to Sandra, "It feels like I've got two young kids and a husband who also needs me to mother him and tell him exactly how to be a more involved dad. If I don't tell him over and over, he just shines it on and doesn't do a thing around the house."

According to Edgar, "I try to help out with dressing the kids sometimes, preparing breakfast three days a week, and loading the dishwasher, but all I get is criticism because I don't do things exactly the way Sandra wants them done."

During their couples counseling, I introduced the idea of tzim-tzum in a healthy marriage (or how to lighten up and make room for each other to bring out their best as copartners). I explored with Sandra how to initiate a Two-Way Teach Me Conversation with Edgar about what would help him be more active in lightening her load at home. This would also help her clarify in her own mind which tasks she wanted to do her way, which tasks she was willing to let Edgar do his way, and which tasks would require some back-and-forth collaboration and teamwork.

Then I explored with Edgar how to lighten up somewhat from the stresses and edginess he brought home each night from work, so he could be more receptive when Sandra was telling him what she needed or preferred. This was helpful for him, because he'd always assumed that if he acted receptive or humble, he would seem wimpy or weak. As a result of a few focused counseling sessions, Edgar was able to start becoming a much stronger, more supportive, and more broad-shouldered partner, which meant he could be receptive and masculine at the same time. Instead of acting like a scolded child or rebellious teenager, he began listening to Sandra's needs and taking her concerns seriously without getting defensive or dismissive as he had done in the past.

Their relationship was tested, however, when Sandra went out of town to spend time with her sick mother. In the past, when she'd had to leave town on business or for a family obligation, Sandra had often stayed up late, preparing everything, several nights beforehand. She feared that unless she made a week's worth of frozen meals and spelled out every detail of what needed to be done in long lists, she could not trust Edgar to do a good job. Then she would resent how "inept" her husband was and get upset when he (intentionally or unintentionally) went against her precise instructions.

This time we took a few minutes to have a calm and proactive Two-Way Teach Me Conversation a week before Sandra was scheduled to go out of town. During this relaxed, creative back-and-forth brainstorming session, Sandra asked Edgar to teach her which things during the upcoming week he might need her to plan or arrange versus those he could comfortably plan and arrange without much input from her. It turned out that Edgar was fully ready to take over 80 percent of the tasks but needed some input from her on the 20 percent for which he knew she had specific and legitimate ways of doing things.

Rather than arguing or letting each other down, they had found a way to be teammates and mutually respectful partners. Sandra discovered that nearly 80 percent of the things she usually exhausted herself arranging ahead of time could be handled just fine by Edgar, and this freed up a lot of her time and energy to do other things in preparation for her intense week of being with her mom. Edgar discovered that he actually enjoyed doing more around the house and being a strong partner for his wife and kids, especially when he wasn't being criticized or micromanaged. This was the beginning of an enormous amount of progress in their marriage, and it renewed their sense of trust and intimacy.

As Sandra admitted later, "By stepping back, finding a way to have Edgar teach me how to bring out the best in him, and not trying to do it all like a resentful martyr, I realized that it's not all on my shoulders. That's a huge relief, and my entire sense of well-being improved once I felt the pressure lifting somewhat."

Edgar explained, "I used to come home completely fried from all the stresses at work. But now I take a few seconds before I walk in the front door and say to myself, 'Tzimtzum. Lighten up, make room for these people you love and who are more important than anyone else you've dealt with during the day.' Just a few moments of breathing calmly and reminding myself what it's all about has made me a much stronger and more successful husband and dad."

STRESSING LESS BUT ACCOMPLISHING MORE

Each of these scenarios shows that it is possible to find a balance between the part of you that wants to rush in and control things and the part of you that needs to pull back and not feel so overloaded and stressed. Whether it's in your home life, your work life, or your involvement in nonprofit groups or social events, you are the only one who will know for sure if you're finding that balance or if you're leaning too far toward doing too much or too little.

Lightening up and allowing others to be your creative partners in life may still be a little scary or unfamiliar to you, especially if your trust has been betrayed in the past. But if the Isaac Luria description of the creation of the world is correct, then even the Creative Source had to pull back somewhat so as not to overwhelm the fragile vessels with too much unfiltered energy all at once. We human beings also need to learn how to create and accomplish things without excessively dominating, controlling, or shattering anyone or anything in our path.

When each of us learns to breathe calmly and make room for all that surrounds us, then we will have discovered a peaceful way to live our lives without harming any of the fragile and remarkable creations that share this world with us. It begins with how we make room for others at home, at work, and in our communities. I hope you will enjoy this process of taking better care of yourself and others by doing a little less and finding that it leads to more health, creativity, and teamwork for everyone involved.

5

Responding with Wisdom When Someone Treats You Harshly

PLEASE PUT ON your seat belts. We're going to be talking about how to handle those stressful moments when you have to deal with a manipulative, insensitive, or verbally aggressive person you encounter at work, in a family situation, or in various social situations and nonprofit activities.

I've found that in nearly every small group, large organization, neighborhood gathering, spiritual community, or extended family, there tends to be at least one person who occasionally blurts out hurtful things toward you or someone you care about deeply. Or one person who tries to throw his or her weight around and doesn't care if you or someone else gets harmed in the process.

This chapter will explore one of the most enlightened and effective ways to respond to harsh or hurtful individuals. We will also discuss how to take good care of your own heart, soul, and sanity when you're face-to-face with someone who intentionally or unintentionally stirs up trouble.

WALKING ON EGGSHELLS

Almost a year ago, Connie came to my office to discuss some of the stresses in her busy life. She was referred by a close friend of mine, who described her as "one of the nicest people on the planet—a genuinely caring, intelligent person with an especially challenging and stressful job in the film business."

After an extremely busy few weeks, Connie felt somewhat exhausted prior to making an appointment for therapy. During her initial counseling session, she told me, "I was hired two years ago to work for a man who is quite brilliant and decent. But, of course, he got fired six months ago, and now I am reporting to a very intense woman who is a bit like Miranda Priestly (the Meryl Streep character in *The Devil Wears Prada*). I've usually gotten along well with women bosses, but this particular executive is definitely the most self-absorbed and demanding person I've ever met. Even though I walk on eggshells each day to make my boss happy, she still finds something that enrages her every few hours. I often feel like I should show up at work wearing a bulletproof jacket to protect myself from her verbal eruptions."

In addition, Connie talked about her verbally abusive ex-husband (they had been separated for more than six months), who had called her with an angry tirade the night before our first session. She commented, "My ex is quite charismatic and handsome. He seems to be able to attract women to him wherever he goes. The problem is that he grew up with an emotionally abusive father, so he's got this defiant, 'no one is ever going to tell me what to do' reaction to anything I say about our daughter, our marital vows, our divorce negotiations, or any other controversial topic. As a result, it's usually all about him, and I worry that our young daughter is going to grow up without the kind of encouragement and daily involvement she deserves from a sensible, loving father."

Connie looked down for a moment near the end of the session and added quietly, "I sometimes feel so drained as a result of having a boss from hell and an ex who's infuriating. I want to learn what I'm doing wrong that I keep attracting these intense, demanding individuals who are so oblivious to my feelings and so caught up in making sure it's all about them. I don't want to spend the rest of my life walking on eggshells and never feeling safe."

Does Connie's situation sound at all like you or someone you know? Have you ever been the target of someone else's emotional outbursts or hurtful remarks? Have you ever wondered why some of the nicest people in the world get saddled daily with stressful interactions with harsh bosses, family members, or difficult partners?

As I told Connie, it's not just the argumentative phone calls and the tense face-to-face interactions with self-absorbed people that can be draining and stressful. You may often feel a lingering discomfort in your stomach, shoulders, or lower back when you are bombarded over and over by people who see you as an object to be manipulated and pressured into doing their bidding. Or you might have agitated thoughts and feelings at night when you try to sleep. Or your mind may be occupied during daylight hours with how you're going to respond next to the unreasonable demands of someone who expects you to jump each time he or she has a pressing urge for your complete attention or loyal compliance.

In Connie's case, she was having trouble sleeping and was frequently tired and impatient as a result of encountering two high-powered individuals who were demanding toward her day after day. The escalating pressures and criticisms she received from her explosive boss and her stubborn ex-husband were sapping her energy.

Think about your own challenges at work, within your family, or in various social situations. Do you ever find the following to be true?

- A few men or women you encounter every so often have an unstoppable sense of urgency that it's always about them.

- There is someone who tends to treat you like a pawn in his or her schemes and power plays.

- There is someone you've spent time with lately who tends to drain you with excessive or exhausting criticism, whining, or verbal abuse.

- There are one or more people in your life who say or do things that make you feel pressured or who give you the sense that if you make one wrong move, they will explode or turn against you.

- You wonder how you became saddled with the job of trying to please a particularly demanding person who is never really pleased or who constantly expects you to put your needs aside and respond to whatever he or she desires.

When you or someone you love are treated badly by a verbally abusive person, it's important to take a few moments to breathe and get some genuine support for how unpleasant it is to be on the receiving end of someone else's repeated harshness. As I offered sincerely to Connie, "I'm so sorry for how exhausting it is to deal each day with your explosive boss and your stubborn ex, who sounds very difficult. It doesn't seem fair that a person like you, who works hard and tries to do the right thing, gets assaulted with so much negativity. In counseling, you and I will need to do all we can to make sure your physical health, your daughter's well-being, and your life in general aren't permanently held back by these toxic interactions with your boss and your ex."

In my office that afternoon, I remember watching Connie take a deep, relaxing breath. Then she said, "Thank you for taking this seriously. I feel as if I need to get my strength back, or I'm not going to be able to take good care of my daughter and myself. I know I've got to be realistic about money, so I have to deal with my agitated boss until I find a better job. Plus, I still have to maintain some contact with my ex-husband as long as we have these shared parenting issues and lots of financial decisions to make. But I wish there were some way to regain my clarity and not feel so wiped out each time I have an unpleasant interaction with these two people."

We spent some more time discussing the fact that Connie deserved a lot of credit for the ways in which she was already taking steps to stand up for her daughter and her own needs. I asked her if she felt ready to take on the next step in the stress-reduction and healing process. She took one more deep breath and said, "I am definitely ready to stop being such a doormat and to start responding in a different way to these tough individuals."

I then offered Connie an easy-to-understand but highly transformative shift in perspective that I learned in my twenties while in a reading group that discussed Jewish spiritual texts. We were studying a well-known book called the Pirke Avot (which tends to be translated as either *Chapters of Essential Principles, Ethics of the Fathers,* or *Sayings of the Ancestors*).[1] The Pirke Avot is a compilation of thought-provoking spiritual advice and practical insights from the most revered teachers who lived approximately nineteen hundred years ago in the towns of Jerusalem, Yavneh, Lod, B'nai B'rak, and other centers of orally transmitted wisdom that expanded dramatically after the destruction of the Second Temple in the year 70 C.E.

WORDS TO SHIFT YOUR PERSPECTIVE

In Chapter 4 of the Pirke Avot, there is a quote from a young, highly respected scholar named Shimon Ben Zoma, who lived in the second century. Ben Zoma taught his students to practice the following daily perspective:[2]

Who is the wise person? The one who learns from each human being.

Imagine for a moment that this brief two-sentence mantra is like a silent and invisible protective shield that keeps you safe, centered, and alert at the moments when someone is barking at you, criticizing you, or trying to intimidate you. Rather than feeling

trapped or powerless when you are around someone who is verbally abusive or physically imposing, you can regain your power
and clarity by taking a gentle, comforting breath and say to yourself, "Who is the wise person? The one who learns from each
human being, because there may be something important and
useful for me to learn here, despite how inappropriately this person
is behaving. Possibly there is some valuable wisdom that is going to
come out of this situation if I stay alert and aware."

This valuable wisdom might be about a part of your psyche that
you have never fully understood or appreciated. Or it might be useful information about how and when to be strong and not let
someone trample your feelings or values. Or it might be subtle
clues as to what your next personal growth challenge will be. To
understand what it means to "learn from each human being,"
please examine some of the illustrations that follow.

PUTTING THIS INTO PRACTICE

As a first step, it's useful to say this Pirke Avot mantra silently to
yourself in the middle of a highly stressful situation. Think about
the skills and calm demeanor you would see in a talented and experienced vice president of customer service, who has to deal gently and helpfully with all sorts of irate customers who vent their
pent-up frustration. An inexperienced or clumsy assistant might
act defensive or dismissive toward an irritated, complaining customer and make things worse. But a skilled customer service prac-
titioner would think confidently, "I can learn from each person."
At the same time, he or she would say calmly and sincerely to the
irate individual, "Tell me exactly what happened. Take your time.
I'm very interested in finding out what occurred and what we can
do to resolve this situation fairly."

Rather than being defensive, dismissive, or argumentative, the
experienced vice president of customer service knows that he or
she has enough power, insight, empathy, integrity, and creativity
to deal with whatever has made the customer so upset. The calm-

ing sense of genuine caring and good listening skills he or she exhibits often causes the customer to gradually slow down a bit and
be less aggressive. In fact, research shows the best way to get an
upset and verbally aggressive individual to lower his or her voice
and stop being so oppressive is to demonstrate clearly that you do
value his or her input and that you are definitely taking him or her
seriously.[3]

This isn't always easy for most people. Sometimes your heart
may be beating rapidly. Your stomach or intestines may be churn-
ing. Your breathing may become shallow or rapid. Your mind may
be racing with possible comeback lines, justifications, or defensive
comments that you wish you could hurl back at the person who's
attacking you. But even though it's not easy, you can still become
the wise, patient person and turn this stressful moment into an opportunity for deep learning and remarkable breakthroughs.

Even if right now it seems a bit unnerving that you would be
able to stay strong and clear the next time someone is bad-mouth-
ing you or someone you care about, I hope you are still willing to
give it a few sincere attempts. For example, imagine for a moment
that you are a lot like the vice president of customer service and
possess many of those same skills to breathe, open your heart, and
listen fully to what an irate or verbally harsh person is saying. It
might be someone at work, in your family, or in a public setting
who aggressively says something unpleasant or contemptuous
about you or someone else.

But instead of getting bent out of shape, you are able to say
quickly and silently to yourself, "Who is the wise person? The one
who learns from each human being." Rather than becoming reactive and reflexive, you can take a deep, relaxing breath; draw on
your inner wisdom; and say to yourself, "I need to learn something here. I need to find out why this person is so distressed, and
I need to explore what I can do to stay calm, centered, and em-
powered in order to deal more effectively with this situation."

Please note that this does not mean you are being a doormat or
a pushover for this irate individual. Rather, you are staying calmly

in your own power and mindfulness (just like a highly talented customer service representative) as you explore what's really happened to cause this verbally abusive individual to start spewing in your direction.

WHAT CAN WE LEARN FROM AN IRRITABLE OR DEMANDING PERSON?

You may be surprised at the deep and useful things you will learn when you put this mindful method of response into practice. In the following sections, we will explore a few possibilities of what is meant by being wise and learning from every person.

Learning about Who You Don't Want to Be

When you are with a boss, a relative, a stranger, or a colleague who is speaking in an irate, accusatory, or self-righteous tone of voice, your first visceral reaction is often, "Yuck. Get me away from this person." Or you might be tempted to want to criticize the person's tone and try to get them to change a long-time habit he or she isn't interested in changing.

But if you silently say to yourself, "Who is the wise person? The one who learns from each human being," you might quickly notice that the irate individual in front of you is using a tone and an attitude that you have occasionally slipped into during your own worst moments. Maybe you don't do it as often as this person or to the same excessive degree, but if you have ever fallen into a similar habit of being whiny, negative, accusatory, arrogant, or verbally self-righteous, now is the moment when you can reach a new level of wisdom and commit to never doing it again.

You can say to yourself silently, "Wow! I now know exactly what it looks and feels like when someone is acting like a self-righteous jerk. Please God (or Inner Strength), don't let me use this person's unpleasant tone of voice ever again. I definitely don't want to act out like this in front of my loved ones. I certainly can't afford to be like this at work. In fact, I don't want to exhibit this kind of tone or attitude with anyone I encounter. I am acutely aware that I am ready to learn whatever it takes to come up with better ways of getting things done than to slip into this kind of ugliness ever again."

In Connie's case, when I asked her if she had ever exhibited (even to a tiny extent) the harshness of her boss or the stubbornness of her ex-husband, she smiled and admitted, "I certainly don't do it as often or as intensely as they do. But sometimes, when I'm especially tired or worn out, a whiny, demanding tone of voice or an agitated impatience comes from my mouth or my nonverbal body language, and it's not who I want to be."

So in preparation for the next time that her boss or ex-husband spoke to her in a demanding or demeaning way, Connie made a promise to herself. She said, "The next time I'm the target of their verbal intensity, I want to learn from it. I want to discover how to make sure that I won't keep slipping back into an ugly tone of voice with my daughter, my colleagues, and my loved ones. I will figure out how to ask for my needs and preferences much earlier in a clear, calm voice—before I get to the edgy place of being tired, whiny, or demanding. I want to learn how to get up the courage to let people know what I'm requesting in a decent and engaging tone of voice as soon as possible rather than remaining silent until the frustration builds up and I come off sounding even remotely like my demanding boss or my stubborn ex-husband."

Have you ever found that at certain times in your own life, when you are exhausted, overloaded, or frustrated, you resort to behaviors that are a little too much like the people you find unpleasant or negative? Do you become a little more short-tempered, whiny, or stubborn than you would like to be? Do you ever come out with a long list of accusations or a self-righteous tone that is a definite turn-off for your kids, your partner, your coworkers, or anyone else who is on the receiving end of your diatribe?

If you are able to say yes to any of these questions, that's a good thing. It means you've taken an important and courageous step toward becoming more insightful by obtaining some important clues from each person who gets on your nerves. This could be the spark that keeps you motivated to treat others exactly the way you would like to be treated.

Learning about an Aspect of Yourself That Is Hidden

Here's a second highly useful possibility to consider whenever someone is being self-absorbed, demanding, or unpleasant. Maybe this person exhibits an excessive amount of some personality trait or behavior that you have been downplaying in yourself or that you have been hiding or suppressing so no one will ever see that side of you. Perhaps this demanding or intense person is revealing in a more intense version an uncomfortable part of yourself that you keep running away from or suppressing.

For example, in Connie's case, I asked her, "What qualities or behaviors do your boss and ex-husband display in excess that you hold back in yourself?" She thought for a moment and then commented, "When I think of the way my boss and my ex are so demanding and I'm so afraid to be too demanding, it feels like I've got myself in a straitjacket, and they're on the opposite extreme letting all their requests and desires burst out all over the place."

I asked her to tell me more about how she felt held back on the issue of being demanding or putting it out there as compared to her ex and her boss. She explained, "If I think about it, I realize that they are both charismatic and capable of creating excitement and enthusiasm for their good ideas. They've both got a lot of energy, and they don't have the same inhibitions or cautiousness that I have about requesting support from others."

Then she admitted, "I sometimes feel a little jealous at how compelling and effective they tend to be when they're passionate and focused about some idea or project. Of course, they tend to go overboard in demanding too much from everyone else, yet I tend to be so worried and self-conscious about being nice or not making waves that I don't allow people to become excited or enthusiastic about the projects and ideas that matter deeply to me. It's as if my boss and my ex have total freedom to make things happen and I've got myself all knotted up with too many restrictions."

This was an important insight for Connie's therapy. Like many of us, she felt victimized by people who tend to be gung ho in a selfish way, and as a result, she held back her own willingness to be passionate and persistent about her most cherished goals and dreams. If this sounds like you or someone you care about, please know that you don't have to become excessively self-absorbed or obnoxiously demanding to raise your level of passion and persistence on important projects in your personal or work life.

I suggested to Connie, "Let's work together to make sure you find the right level of intensity to get people to rally in support of your goals and ideas without going over the line into selfishness or disrespect for others' feelings and needs." To help her shift away from being a person who passively watched self-absorbed people steal the spotlight, I asked, "On a scale of one to ten, with one representing no charisma or never shining brightly and ten representing an excessive amount of charisma and demanding too much attention, where would you rank yourself, your boss, and your ex-husband?"

She took a moment to consider the range of scores and then replied, "I guess I'm way down at one or two with little or no charisma or bright light shining, because I'm usually afraid of letting anyone know what I'm passionate about. My boss and my ex-husband are up at nine or ten, because they're constantly insisting that everyone get on board with what they think is important or valuable."

Then I asked, "To do a better job of standing up for your daughter and getting support for the projects you care about at work, where would you like to be on the charisma/light-shining scale?"

Connie quickly knew what she wanted: "I certainly don't want to become a narcissist or an insufferable nine or ten like my boss or my ex. But I definitely should raise my level up to maybe five or six, so I can be a more effective advocate for my daughter and for my projects."

During the next several weeks of counseling, Connie and I developed a series of action steps she could take to boost her level of charisma and willingness to shine. We explored her personal sense of what constituted being too demanding and not being demanding enough. We discussed what specific words and tones of voice felt respectful and compassionate when asking for support versus what might cause a listener to feel diminished, trampled, manipulated, or disrespected.

We also explored Connie's feelings and preferences about what she wore, how she spoke up at meetings, how passionately she might follow through on a stalled project, and how she networked behind the scenes to boost the chances of success for work projects and her daughter's education. As she admitted, "I don't want to dress up like a spoiled fashionista, but I also don't want to keep dressing down like some invisible, inconsequential person who can easily be overlooked. Nor do I want to keep my good ideas locked inside and let others dominate the important meetings and decisions. I'm definitely in the mood for putting my ideas out there in a professional and sensible manner."

Each week in my office, we made sure to talk about exactly how Connie could keep sight of her strong sense of empathy, humility, and decency to guarantee that she would not become narcissistic or insufferable like her boss or her ex. She found that over the next several weeks and months she made significant progress in becoming more persistent, energetic, visible, respected, and successful at getting things done in a manner that generated enthusiasm and support from others. Instead of being an overly nice and compassionate wallflower at one or two on the charisma/light-shining scale, Connie gradually raised her profile and her persistence level to the five or six level that helped her get much better results.

As you think about someone in your own life who is narcissistic, demanding, excessive, or unstoppable, please take a moment each time you are around this person to ask yourself a few crucial questions:

- Instead of passively resenting this person or feeling bowled over by him or her, what if I could embody some of the same engaging, intense energy and persistence to use for good purposes in my own life and goals?

- What if I gave myself permission to boost the specific quality in myself that I have been afraid might make me behave like him or her, but in fact I could boost this quality in myself from a low 1 or 2 to an excellent 5 or 6 without even getting close to the excessive 8 or 9 that makes this person so insufferable?

- What specific new behaviors, coaching sessions, and ongoing support will I need to raise my effectiveness with this trait that I have been blocking or hiding from for a long time?

Please note that I am not advising you to become self-absorbed, excessively demanding, or insensitive to others. I am suggesting that sometimes we can benefit from seeing how passionate and persistent other intense individuals tend to be when they pursue their goals and dreams. We can learn from each human being how to fire up the commitment, the resourcefulness, and most important, the compassion and decency we can choose to bring to our own cherished projects. We probably can also be a lot more balanced and graceful about it than the extreme individuals who are so indifferent to the needs and feelings of others.

CLUES TO HOW TO DEFUSE
THE VOLATILE PERSON

As I said earlier, the goal in being mindful and learning from each human being is not to become a doormat or a passive victim. In fact, if you silently say the focusing phrase "Who is the wise person? The one who learns from each human being," it will help you to feel centered and strong enough to see clearly what works and what doesn't to bring out the best possible interactions with a difficult individual.

In Connie's case, after a few weeks of trying out this perspective, she became quite successful at staying calm, centered, and creative when she dealt with her self-absorbed, volatile boss and ex-husband. From this place of centered clarity, she was then able to notice some important clues about what worked and what didn't in managing the explosive moods of these two edgy people.

As she explained in one of her most crucial therapy sessions, "I can finally see what I've been doing that makes things worse with my boss. I noticed this week that my boss gets most upset whenever she feels contradicted or unsupported in front of other people. In private, she can engage in some healthy back-and-forth exchange of ideas. But if there are other people in the room, especially any of the other back-stabbing executives she is always trying to compete with and impress, you can see her tense up. If someone at a meeting or social event disagrees with her or questions her judgment, I can see a flush of redness flare up on the back of her neck, and her jaw becomes extremely tight, as though she's about to crack or lash out. But if she and I find a way to be aligned and mutually supportive as we go into a meeting or other event, she can be quite charming, playful, and delightful."

As a result of these insights, Connie began to take an extra few moments before every meeting or public event to say to her boss in a quick, one-on-one aside, "Hey, let's synchronize our goals here so we can back each other up. Tell me what you want to see happen in the next few minutes and what you want to make sure doesn't go wrong. I want this to go well for us."

She noticed over the next few weeks that when she brought this soothing and professional team-building tone to their conversations, her boss began to treat her as a trusted and valued partner: "Each time we had one of these quick, proactive, synchronizing moments a few minutes or hours before a stressful meeting, I could see her jaw and her face relax somewhat. She's still a piece of work, but she no longer seems to view me as a threat when I take the time for a private conversation to clarify our sense of team-work. Instead of turning against me or lashing out at me for con-tradicting her in front of other people, she has begun to share more of her thoughts with me, and she has actually started to lis-ten to some of my good ideas—as long as I share them with her one-on-one when no one would be able to see that she is not all-knowing and all-powerful."

With Connie's ex-husband, a completely different strategy turned out to be the winning approach: "I'm starting to see that my ex is a bully who definitely enjoys intimidating people with his demeaning comments and manipulative games. But I noticed when I began to watch him closely in a scientific, detached way that if someone stops him playfully, calmly, or professionally right at the moment when he's starting to dominate, he pulls back and avoids a direct confrontation. Like many bullies, he seems to get a pleasurable rush if he sees you're feeling trapped or resentful as a result of his pushiness, yet he's not very adept if someone calmly and unemotionally stands up to him. If someone smiles calmly and says, 'I don't agree,' or 'Hey, that's not okay. Let's have a do-over and find something that works better for both of us,' he tends to become silent and unsure of what to do. I saw it happen in a few different settings."

As a result of these observations, Connie began to try some-thing she had never attempted before. She explained, "Now when he starts to get demanding or pushy during a phone call or a face-to-face conversation, I simply take a breath, stay centered, and say gently, 'Hey, time out. You've got a legitimate point of view, and I'm going to make sure your concerns get taken seriously here. So you go first and let me know what you'd like in this situation. Then I want you to listen for just a moment to my concerns as well, so we can come up with a solution that works for both of us.'

"This calm, confident, and professional tone of voice from me tends to catch him off guard. He's used to me getting emotional or silently building up resentment. When I respond comfortably with this unflappable but in-charge tone, he seems to stop dominating for a moment and even calms down a bit. Maybe it's because he knows he's going to be heard and taken seriously, even if he's going to have to listen to my needs as well."

Watching for Clues in Your Most Challenging Interactions

If you want to be more effective with a boss, coworker, customer, roommate, relative, neighbor, or other individual who tends to be intense or verbally abusive at times, please take a moment to pay attention to what seems to calm this person and what seems to provoke his or her most anxious or demanding qualities. You can benefit immediately by asking yourself (or others who know the person well) these questions:

- What settings, words, tone of voice, and nonverbal gestures seem to trigger this person's anger or defensiveness?

- What settings, words, tone of voice, or subtle gestures seem to bring out the most cooperative, intelligent, or relaxed behavior in this person?

- What self-soothing statements will you say to yourself during your next interaction with this sometimes-harsh individual?

- What calming, playful, and professional words and tone of voice will you use the next time you notice this person getting edgy, bossy, or demanding?

These questions can be extremely helpful from both a scientific and a spiritual perspective. If you imagine yourself to be a social scientist (maybe an anthropologist observing an interesting but unusual subculture), you can watch this agitated individual from a safe and professional distance. When you put yourself in the role of a scientist, this person is no longer dangerous or intimidating; rather, he or she becomes fascinating, interesting, complicated, and worth watching closely to learn how to bring out the best in him or her.

From a spiritual perspective, when you take a breath, regain your center, and open to the wisdom of learning from each human being, you are essentially searching for the hidden spark of holy light that Jewish spirituality claims can be found in every living being.[4] Now I'll admit that in some individuals it's not easy to find that spark. It sometimes gets covered over by many layers of unprocessed traumatic experiences, unpleasant personality traits, repetitive defense mechanisms, and sneaky ways of saving face that make it hard to find the true inner essence. It might take years or decades before you are able to sift through all those layers of irritating behaviors and traits to find a remarkable, wounded child or a precious, vulnerable soul hidden deep inside that agitated human being.

But when you combine the scientific search for what works and the spiritual search for the inner spark of light, you are likely to be more successful at staying calm and centered during each interaction with a challenging person. Yes, you will still have moments during which this person's rage or sneakiness gets on your nerves. But when you take a deep breath and remind yourself that you are becoming wiser in many ways by having the opportunity to learn and grow as a result of your exchanges with this individual, it sometimes gets easier.

You might actually find yourself admitting silently, "If it weren't for this extremely challenging person testing me so often, I don't know if I'd be as motivated to learn and grow as much as I have recently." I'm not recommending that you send this person a Hallmark card that says, "Thank you for being so difficult. You forced me to learn and grow far beyond anyone else." But I am suggesting that you take a moment every so often to give yourself credit for your persistence, your insightfulness, and each small step of progress you have made in staying healthy even while having to deal with such a challenging individual.

6

Being Open to a Hidden Gift in the Most Distressing Moments

THE PHONE RINGS. It's upsetting news. Someone is seriously ill or dying; something tragic has happened; a much-needed job has ended abruptly; or a good solution to a lingering problem is suddenly no longer a possibility.

Your heart races. Your thoughts are jumbled. Your body tenses up. You're not sure what to do first. The world around you seems to go on with its usual rhythms as though nothing much has happened. But for you or someone you care about, the old "normal" is gone. The painful news has shaken you profoundly.

What can you say to yourself at upsetting moments like these? What can you call on from deep inside that might make a crucial difference? How do you regain your strength, clarity, and creativity in the middle of a painful loss or a crushing disappointment?

These are a few of the questions we will explore in this chapter. But I need to warn you that this topic is controversial. In Jewish spirituality, there is a fascinating phrase that says, "Gam zu l'tovah. Even this could become for the good." Blurted out at the wrong moment, it can be perceived as a hurtful and insensitive remark that will cause others to pull away from you.

However, when uttered at the right moment with genuine humility and compassion, this phrase can work wonders for reducing stress or overload, as well as transforming a traumatic or upsetting situation into a source of healing and creative beauty. I have found in my own life (and in those of many people with whom I have spoken) that something unexpected and positive can occur as a result of meditating on these particular words.

Please be careful how you use this reenergizing phrase. It is not meant to suppress or interrupt the important process of grieving for a major loss. Nor is it meant to be a mindless, superficial bandage that tries to cover a deep and significant wound. I've found that many people tend to be clumsy or unintentionally hurtful when they use this phrase incorrectly. In this chapter, I'm going to start with the positive results I've repeatedly seen people achieve from using this inspiring remedy. I urge you to stick around, however, to hear the important warnings about the frequent misuses of this phrase at the end of the chapter.

FROM HELPLESSNESS TO CREATIVE OPENNESS

This particular phrase has a long history that has been documented extensively.[1] During the Roman Empire in the first century in Israel, there was an acclaimed teacher named Rabbi Nachum. He was the mentor for many brilliant students, including Rabbi Akiva, who became one of the most respected scholars in Judaism and is still studied today throughout the world.[2]

Rabbi Nachum had several physical, financial, and personal setbacks to deal with in his life. Yet he often said the following phrase to himself when there was a painful loss, a tough challenge, or a huge disappointment:

Gam zu l'tovah. Even this could become for the good.

Some people in the twenty-first century (where snarkiness and cynicism are often the norm) would probably accuse Rabbi Nachum of being naïve, blissed out, or in denial. But if you understand the deeper, hidden levels of what this phrase means, it stops being a happy-talk slogan and starts to become a courageous and profound call to action, creativity, and healing instead.

I'll give you a brief summary of the huge number of ways this mantra can be transformative during a stressful crisis or in the middle of a tragic situation.

The Rebelliousness of These Words

Because my father grew up in the 1930s in a medium-sized town called Plauen in Germany and many of my relatives died in the Holocaust, I've always been fascinated by how various men and women were stubborn enough to keep their dignity and integrity intact, even during some of the most horrific circumstances in human history. As I mentioned in the introduction to this book, I was inspired during my college years by the books and teachings of Dr. Viktor Frankl that told how he made sure his humor, rebelliousness, compassion, and decency stayed alive, even while his body was close to death in Auschwitz.[3] No matter how cynical and cruel the people around him became, Frankl somehow found a way to choose a different point of view and try to find at least one opportunity each day to be of service and do something compassionate or useful.

Several years ago I had the opportunity to counsel an aging survivor of the concentration camps—a smart and irrepressible Jewish woman in her seventies, who was struggling with a horrible illness that was taking away her mobility and her independence. I remember looking into this woman's intense eyes and asking her, "What do you say to yourself each morning to give yourself the strength to carry on?"

She smiled a mischievous smile and explained, "I'm very stubborn and defiant. If someone tries to take away my freedom or my humanity, I dig in my heels and make sure they are not able to control my thoughts and actions. I remember, when I was a little girl, my grandfather used to say whenever something horrible or painful was happening to us, 'Gam zu l'tovah. Even this might eventually be turned into something good.' Saying those words defiantly and silently in my most distressing moments have taken me out of a place of helplessness and passivity. What I've learned in my life is that even when my mobility or physical health is compromised, I can still passionately hold on to my deepest values and look carefully for ways to do something positive and helpful. That's something no one will ever take away from me."

I think of this woman often when things are difficult in my own life. I envision her when she was a teenager in the concentration camps or as an aging grandma in my office. I bring to mind her playful smile as she responded defiantly to the tragic moments in her life and said silently, "I will continue to look for ways to emerge from hopelessness and helplessness. Gam zu l'tovah. I will find a way to turn *even this* into something that has compassion or goodness."

The Creativity of These Words

Sometimes when you say, "Gam zu l'tovah. Even this could possibly be for good," it reminds you to spend a few unrushed minutes or hours connecting with something creative or beautiful. It might involve taking precious time during an otherwise upsetting day to look at a few exquisite works of art or spending a few delicious minutes gardening or walking in nature. Or it might be taking a deep breath as you listen to an inspiring piece of music or read a thought-provoking book or article. Or you might need to spend some nourishing time creating art, music, or written pages of your own that express what you are going through at that moment.

Instead of shutting down or numbing out as a result of your distressing situation, the silent words "Gam zu l'tovah. Even this could possibly be for good" can suddenly make you remember to bring something inspiring or vibrant into your field of vision. It doesn't make the pain go away entirely, but it lifts you up to a vantage point from which you can see new possibilities for a glimmer of healing, decency, insight, or beauty to emerge from an upsetting situation.

For example, my wife, Linda, is an artist. Even during the toughest moments in her life, she is usually able to renew her vitality and inner strength when she's out in nature or involved in something artistic or creative. Last year, when Linda was suddenly diagnosed with cancer, I thought at first it would cause her to shut down and become fearful. But within a few hours of receiving her upsetting news, she was out taking a walk at sunset and marveling at the beauty of the gold, orange, pink, and purple rays emerging in the early evening sky. Rather than shutting down in anxiety or anticipation, she was able to talk about her concerns and her complicated decisions, not from a place of helplessness, but from a deep appreciation of life's beauty and mystery.

Like many creative individuals, Linda knew on some level that before, during, and after her cancer surgery, she needed to be inspired by exquisite works of art and awesome natural scenes that could nourish her soul and strengthen her resilience. During the weeks following her diagnosis, she began taking more walks than usual in public gardens, along the water a few miles from our home, and in neighborhoods where the flowers are fragrant. She put together an inspiring collage of photos and visual images. She also made sure to talk with several of her closest friends who had been through tough cancer challenges of their own.

It's now fourteen months since her surgery, and Linda is cancer free. I am grateful for that and also for how much she has taught me about the importance of looking at art, nature, sunrises, and sunsets, even during the stressful and uncertain times of medical appointments and waiting for results. We often can't control a substantial portion of what happens to our fragile bodies, but we can control how we keep our creativity and vitality alive when dark storm clouds hover around us.

Is there some inspiring piece of music, a few captivating paintings or sculptures, an exquisite walk outdoors, a particularly relaxing place, or a supportive community gathering near where you live that can transform (somewhat but not completely) a trauma or tragedy you have experienced recently? Is there some creative process you enjoy or some other highly expressive activity that tends to reawaken your soul or reopen your appreciation for life and future possibilities?

As I have found many times with Linda and in conversations with my counseling clients and friends, the tough decisions and numerous added stresses of dealing with a challenging crisis (while still going to work and putting food on the table) are much easier to handle when they are done along with a beautiful connection to nature, music, art, spirituality, or companionship from genuine friends and supportive loved ones. It's common to want to isolate yourself or to close down during a distressing setback. But please ask yourself right now or the next time you face an especially tough situation where there is uncertainty or loss, "What creative elements could I connect with to help give me strength and comfort during these stressful times? What can I do to turn *even this* in the direction of healing, creative expression, and goodness rather than losing sight of these possibilities?"

Not Knowing but Still Trusting

One of the additional things I like about the phrase "Gam zu l'tovah. Even this could possibly be for the good" is that it has a humble openness and a gentle curiosity about it. The Hebrew words have a rather Zen-like equanimity about them, as you essentially say to yourself, "I am going to breathe calmly and keep my heart open to all the various possibilities, even though I am witnessing a lot of pain and distress right now." Rather than reacting abruptly with a sense of panic or impatience to an upsetting event, you are able to step back and say gently, "I am open to something positive happening somewhere down the road, even if I don't know what that might be or how soon it might occur."

This may not be easy if you tend to be a person who likes things to be resolved quickly. To step back and keep your heart open when your world has been turned upside down does not come automatically for most people. But when you silently and calmly say, "Gam zu l'tovah. Even this could possibly be for the good," it helps you to slow down and not expect immediate results to occur. Because to be honest, we often don't know exactly why something horrible happens or how long the pain and chaos will last. From our limited human perspective, we frequently don't understand why a tragic or painful situation happens to a good person or how long it will take him or her to get on solid footing again.

At a moment when superficial explanations simply cannot begin to fathom the unfairness or the suffering that has taken place, I've found that when I say the "Gam zu l'tovah" mantra to myself, it usually slows down the adrenaline rush and inner agitation. At the same time, this phrase usually helps to stimulate my curiosity about the big-picture viewpoint and the awe-inspiring levels of the universe that I can't see with my own eyes or fully understand from the narrow perspective of being human. And let's face it—no matter how smart or well-read you are, being human means not having the ability to see the entire big picture.

In Judaism, various scholars and rabbis offer several different theories on what might be the big picture when extremely painful things happen to essentially good people. What all of these theories have in common is that they are humble enough to admit, "We humans don't have all the answers"; yet at the same time, these profound theories and metaphors can empower us to act with kindness and wisdom during life's painful moments.

Specifically, Jewish spirituality looks at the possibility of something healing or positive emerging eventually as a result of even the most terribly painful experiences in at least three different ways. As you read these somewhat contradictory explanations, you can decide for yourself which one you like best or whether you might feel drawn to more than one of these possibilities.

Possibility 1: Connecting with the Ultimate Creator of Intense and Somewhat Random Natural Phenomena. The first explanation from many Jewish teachers and writings is the Hasidic view that the world is broken, fragmented, and in need of repair because of the shattering (at the moment of creation) of the vessels that couldn't contain all the holy light from an unlimited Source.[4] This widely discussed, sixteenth-century theory from Rabbi Isaac Luria of Safed, which is in many ways similar to the big bang theory of twentieth-century physics, was described earlier in chapter 4. Luria's theory suggests that to create a physical world that wouldn't continually shatter from so much unfiltered light and energy, the Eternal One had to pull back somewhat and make room for creation to emerge. *Tzimtzum* is the Hebrew word for pulling back or making room, and according to Luria, we live in a world where the shattered vessels of physical and emotional creation need to be repaired (a process that he called *tikkun olam,* which means "repairing the world").

So when there is an earthquake, a tornado, a hurricane, a violent crime, a toxic chemical spill, a car accident, or a human tragedy, it is a natural extension of the fact that the unlimited and ever-present Creative Source has infused the world to include many layers of filtered energy, which means there are also numerous possibilities for brokenness, chaos, randomness, independence, and free choice that need to be handled with wisdom and caring. To let the many millions of creative elements in the world express themselves and have some individual flexibility, the ever-flowing Source of energy had to restrain Itself somewhat to make room (rather than controlling everything and leaving no room for human free will or natural randomness). This allows for all sorts of complicated and sometimes painful events to occur, especially when stubborn humans or wild, natural elements slip out of alignment from the flow of positive energy of the universe.

Our task as humans is not to give up on life or our longing for connection with the Ultimate Source during distressing moments, but we must rather see that the shifting tectonic plates, wild winds, volatile ocean tides, and impulsivity of human emotions all come from an infinite and unlimited Creative Source that constantly gives us clues and information about how to live in harmony with nature and human volatility.

According to this theory of how the world works, when a tragedy happens or a tough situation arises, we have the opportunity to call out and listen deeply to an unlimited Source of Wisdom so we can align ourselves with what it has been teaching us to do to repair this fragile world (if we have truly been listening). Instead of becoming embittered when there are tragedies or injustices, we must use these moments to reconnect with the holy wisdom we have received throughout history from a compassionate Source.

I remember after the disruptive and devastating 1994 earthquake in Los Angeles, some people in the media were asking, "Where was God?" and "Why do the innocent suffer?" Rabbi Harold Schulweis (whose congregation is a few miles from the quake's epicenter) wrote a beautiful, scientific, and spiritual newspaper article about how we need to respect that the world's randomness, natural disasters, and especially our own free will (including our reluctance to listen to warnings about where and where not to build cities) are part of the original explosive creation of the fragile world and the original un-formed chaos that we are still trying to understand and repair.[5]

Our job as humans is to support one another through turbulent events and to learn all we can about how to live in harmony with the deeper, holy wisdom of the Creative Source, so we can prevent or reduce the damage from future quakes, human conflicts, and other emergency situations. The closer we get to the truth about how the world works and how it can be appreciated for the amazing and diverse creation that it is, the more we will be aligned with the unlimited and infinite Source of Creation that constantly reveals clues and valuable information about how to live peacefully with all that exists.

Possibility 2: Opening Up to the Unseen Levels. A second explanation of why painful things happen to many of us is that what we see and experience on earth is not the whole story. In Jewish spirituality, there are unseen levels of existence where the other side of the story would certainly make sense—if we could somehow fully perceive or understand these unseen levels.[6] From the narrow point of view of the current week or year, an event can seem tragic, horrific, or terribly unfair. Yet from the point of view of infinity and the huge number of centuries that the world has been (and still is) continually developing toward its highest purpose, we need to admit humbly that maybe there is something holy or good taking place that we cannot understand from our self-interested perspective.

For example, when a person dies, many traditional Jews tend to say, "Baruch Dayan Ha'emet," which means "Blessed is the one true Judge" or "Blessed is the One who Expresses the Ultimate Truth." It refers to a big-picture truth or a sense of balance, justice, order, and timelessness that is far bigger than what our eyes can see or our limited human brains can analyze.[7] According to this traditional spiritual belief, you may feel upset about a loss and how unfair it seems. You deserve to be treated lovingly and patiently as you go through the stages of loss and grief. Yet at the same time, there may also exist, on some other level of existence, a corresponding reality in which this painful current loss occurs for a very good reason that you may never know or understand. What if this painful loss is actually opening up the possibility for some new insight or commitment to repairing the world? What if this tragedy can be turned into something that will help to save many other lives in the long run?

One thought-provoking example cited by many teachers and writers from both the Orthodox and Hasidic traditions within Judaism is that when a child or young adult dies, it feels extremely wrong and unfair.[8] Yet these scholars humbly speculate that it may also be that a young person with a short, inspiring life came here for a specific purpose (maybe to touch someone else's life in a positive way, to open someone's heart, to bring certain people together, to provoke a crucial charity or healing project, or to stir up awareness for an important cause). Having fulfilled his or her essential soul purpose, this young person no longer needed to stay.

This is a tough concept for many people to embrace, especially during a painful loss or crisis. Yet what if there really are multiple levels of reality where karma, unseen causalities, essential soul purposes, or big-picture breakthroughs occur beyond what our five senses can comprehend?

In Judaism, you are encouraged to grieve, to express anger (even at God),[9] to tear a piece of clothing to let others know that you feel shattered for a while, and to say from a place of humble belief, "I do not know the ways of the Eternal. But I am open to the possibility that the ultimate truth is intact, that the Source of Goodness is operating on many levels I may never fully understand." It takes a lot of humility and a substantial leap of faith to be able to say in the middle of your anger and grief, "There is so much about this world and this tragedy that I will never fully understand. All I can do is bless the hard-to-comprehend Creative Source that is sorting things out on levels far beyond my cognitive abilities."

It may surprise you to know that the concept of opening up to unseen levels can also be found in one of the most frequently recited, widely revered prayers in all branches of Judaism. In the well-known Kaddish prayer that nearly every Jew recites after the death of a loved one, on the anniversary of a loved one's passing, or to mark the end of each section of a traditional prayer service, there is a fascinating sentence written in Aramaic (which was the everyday, from-the-heart, familiar language spoken by the ancient people of Israel). It says, "Let the name of the Holy One be glorified, exalted, and honored, though God is beyond all the praises, songs, and adorations we can utter."[10]

In other words, even during a holy moment of intense prayer, when we are uttering all the right words, songs, and adoring concepts, we still need to be humble and admit that the Eternal One is beyond whatever box, category, or idea we think captures what God is. Whenever we say the Kaddish prayer with deep sincerity and understanding, we gently remind ourselves not to think that we've mastered the mystery of who or what created the world but rather to connect lovingly with this indefinable One that is beyond our comprehension. From that place of humility and unquenchable curiosity, we may then be able to say during a moment of great pain or distress, "Blessed is the ultimate Truth."

Possibility 3: Appreciating that We All Have Limits. Finally, a third explanation of why bad things happen is offered by many Jewish teachers and rabbis and is noticeably different from the other two. As described in the bestselling book *When Bad Things Happen to Good People* by Rabbi Harold Kushner, many of life's most painful events (such as the tragic death of Kushner's son at a very young age) are not the will of God, because God in this particular theory is believed to be somewhat limited by the very nature of God's essence.

According to Kushner, our losses are a genuine tragedy for which the loving Creative Presence that we call God grieves with us and gives us support to turn it into something positive and healing for others. Kushner writes,[11]

> I believe in God. But I do not believe the same things that I did years ago when I was growing up or when I was a theological student. God does not cause our misfortunes. Some are caused by bad luck, some are caused by bad people, and some are simply an inevitable consequence of our being human and being mortal, living in a world of inflexible natural laws. I can worship a God who hates suffering but cannot eliminate it. We can turn to God for help in overcoming a tragedy precisely because God is as outraged by it as we are. The question is not "Why did this happen to me? What did I do to deserve this." A better question would be,

"Now that this has happened to me, what I am I going to do about it?"

As a nineteenth-century Hasidic rabbi once put it, "Human beings are God's language." God shows opposition to cancer and birth defects not by eliminating them or making them happen only to bad people, but by summoning from friends and neighbors the support and love to ease the burden and to fill the emptiness. God may not prevent the calamities, but God gives us the strength and the perseverance to overcome it.

Many scholars call Kushner's belief system "process theology," because it focuses more on the process of how God's energies function in the world and how God changes over time as a result of what happens in the world of God's creations.[12] In this belief system, there is a mutual dependence between the Creative Source and humans. According to Kushner and others, God needs humans to carry out the loving acts of kindness and repair that cannot be done without our involvement. We need God to bring out the best in us and to give us the strength to follow through on our task of being God's hands and language here on earth.

PUTTING THIS INTO PRACTICE

You might believe, like Isaac Luria and many others, that an unlimited Source had to pull back to make room for free will but that this infinitely expressive Source is still alive around and within us. Or you might believe, like many traditional and mystical rabbis and teachers, that there are unseen levels of reality we cannot perceive from our limited human awareness; yet we can still remain open to the possibility of something good or necessary eventually emerging on various levels of existence from even the most distressing situations here on earth. Or you might believe, like Harold Kushner, that a compassionate but partially limited God grieves with us and inspires us to do good in response to suffering, even when our hearts are broken. Or you might believe something altogether different about why there is so much suffering in the world and how to respond with compassion.

Yet for each of these belief systems, the crucial questions discussed in nearly every different version of Jewish spirituality are as follows:

- Along with your awareness of how much you can't possibly know or can't fully control about a painful situation, are you willing to take action on what you still can influence and turn in a positive direction?

- Are you willing to take specific steps to treat yourself and others with even more caring and wisdom as a result of the painful things you've experienced?

- Are you willing to keep pursuing light, goodness, justice, fairness, and healing, even though you have witnessed severe pain, unfairness, or disappointment?

CAUTIONS ABOUT USING THESE WORDS WITH YOURSELF OR OTHERS

Now we arrive at some of the warnings I mentioned earlier. If saying, "Gam zu l'tovah. Even this could possibly be for the good," seems as if it might be helpful during a moment of distress or deep sadness, please feel free to say it silently to yourself. But if you feel that it is far too soon or much too optimistic to use this phrase when you truly just need to collapse and rest, I encourage you to do whatever is most respectful of your own journey toward healing. Don't rush yourself if you need some unstructured time to do nothing or very little for a while. Sometimes the best repair strategy after an upsetting tragedy, trauma, or disappointment is to take the pressure off for a few hours, days, or weeks.

In addition, I sincerely hope you will think twice before speaking these words out loud to anyone (and more often than not, please refrain from blurting out this phrase to someone else who is going through a painful experience). It could be perceived as extremely awkward or insensitive if you were to go up to someone who's grieving or has suffered a painful loss and say, "Hey don't worry, even this will be for good." Not only does it destroy any credibility you might have with this person, but it also tramples on that person's right to choose his or her own timetable for dealing with grief.

I remember a grieving widow who came to my office a few years ago and told me, "I was shocked last week. It was only a few hours since my beloved husband's funeral, and this woman I barely knew came up to me and insisted with complete certainty, 'Don't worry. It's all good. You'll be dating again in no time at all.' I didn't know whether to laugh or cry at such an insensitive remark. I'm glad I didn't have a drink in my hand, because I might have tossed it in her face."

Think about your own experiences of loss or disappointment. Have you ever felt violated or upset because someone bombarded you much too quickly with advice, insensitive comments, or superficial clichés that made things worse? Or have you ever made the mistake of saying something well intended and prematurely positive to a devastated person who wasn't quite ready to hear what you were offering?

If you want to prevent "foot-in-mouth disease," it's probably a good idea just to listen to what someone in distress wants to tell you. It may be more loving and sensible to say little and simply let this person know that you truly care and are willing to be of service whenever he or she needs help with chores, shopping, or a sympathetic ear.

In Los Angeles, there was recently a horrible tragedy in which a bright and talented young woman was hit by a car and killed while crossing the street to catch a bus. Her mother witnessed the accident, as did many of this remarkable teenager's friends.

At the funeral service, there was a huge crowd of devastated relatives, neighbors, friends, and classmates. The rabbi showed humility and caring as he spoke to the audible sounds of crying in the room. He said gently, "At such a time of grief, what can anyone say to give comfort to those who mourn? In truth, there are no words that can explain or any statement that can ease the depth of our pain.

"Please do not attempt to give meaning to this tragedy. Do not explain that it was God's will, or that it is for the best, or that the good die young, or that there is some kind of purpose to this, because I think those phrases make a mockery of the hurt we feel. Instead say only this: you are not alone. We love you. Your pain breaks my heart. Please know that I will be there for you."[13]

At this intense moment, the mother of the deceased came forward, clutching a piece of artwork that her daughter had created. She said, "To hold her and touch her, I'm wrapping my hands around her artwork. Her hands formed this, so if I hold on to it, I am touching her hands. I struggled to be worthy of being the mother of this unbelievable creature. It was something that was beyond any gift I could have expected."

In response to the large outpouring of care and concern that occurred after this horrible tragedy, the mother told someone privately, "I feel as if God blinked on the morning of the accident, but when He opened His eyes and saw what had happened, He immediately sent people to carry the family through this tragedy."

Maybe in a few days, weeks, or years, the family will begin asking, "How do we turn this horrible loss into something holy that honors our daughter's memory? How can we further sanctify the life of this beloved human being whom we will always miss terribly?" Rushing up prematurely to any of the grieving relatives with phrases like "Gam zu l'tovah. Even this could possibly be for good" is probably not a good idea, because only the family and friends can decide when and how to ask these questions and what kinds of answers they each feel are supportive or insufficient.

Rather than saying these words to a mourning friend or relative, it might be more effective to find a way to become one of the possibilities of goodness that emerges from a tragedy. Offering your assistance, caring, and love (without any clichés or platitudes) is often the best way to come through for someone in a time of crisis or sadness. Then at a later time, that individual may look back and realize, "Even during a horrible moment when everything looked so bleak, there were specific people who reminded me by their actions that there is still goodness and love in the world."

WHAT KINDS OF HIDDEN GIFTS MAY EMERGE?

As you gradually recover from a painful loss or tragedy, it may take a long time before you begin to feel somewhat whole again. To reduce your stress levels and increase your resilience during this slow, step-by-step recovery process, it helps to have some creative ideas in the back of your mind of what might be possible even after a tragedy, a painful loss, or a severe disappointment. As you explore the various examples that follow, notice which ones seem to generate good ideas for bringing a dose of healing to a painful situation that has happened to you (or someone you care about).

The Gift of Preventing Additional Suffering

After something distressing or tragic happens, our minds often feel blank as to what could possibly be a positive way of responding to such a calamity. Please don't worry if your first response is a sense of emptiness or confusion. That's a normal first emotion when your world has been turned upside down.

But as soon as you begin to feel curious, one of the best places to look for a positive response is to ask yourself, "Can I find some information or a clue as to how the world works from this painful incident? Can I do something that might prevent or lessen similar suffering to someone else in the future? Might this terrible loss hold within it a clue that can be helpful for one, two, or many people in the future?"

If you explore these questions on your own or with a supportive friend or advisor, you may be surprised at some of the lifesaving or tragedy-preventing ideas you will discover. The most fascinating and useful ideas may occur to us when our hearts are broken, our routines have been upended, and we're ready to try something new.

For example, someone I have known for many years lost his beloved brother as the result of an unexpected fall from a steep overhang on a wilderness hiking trail. As my friend described it, "One minute my brother was alive, happy, and doing the thing he loved most. Then in the next moment he was gone, and it left so many of us feeling devastated and questioning everything about life."

We eventually found out that despite the fact that my friend's brother was a passionate and experienced hiker, there was a dangerous, unmarked spot on this particular trail that had resulted in several painful injuries and three deaths over the past ten years.

A few weeks after his brother died, my friend was taken over by a feeling of depression and cynicism. He told me, "I feel like I'm sinking into a deep sense of bitterness and isolation, which I don't want to happen."

So I asked him, "If your brother were alive today, what would he do about the fact that this unmarked spot is causing harm to even some adept and experienced hikers?"

He looked up and replied, "My brother would definitely take this seriously and shake things up until each of those hard-to-assess spots was either repaired or clearly marked."

It took a few more weeks and a few more conversations, but my friend began to emerge from his sense of bitterness and isolation. In fact, for the next fourteen months he did several things to honor his brother's memory and prevent future harm to other hikers. He first got up the courage to visit the exact location of his brother's death in order to photograph and diagram exactly where the danger was and to interview some nearby hikers who had narrowly escaped the same tragic fate. Then he lobbied several key organizations to make sure sufficient warning markers and trail repairs could prevent future accidents. Finally, he began raising money for a nonprofit organization that takes low-income teens into the wilderness to enjoy the beauty of nature and the life lessons that can be gained from exploring the wild spaces most people rarely get to see.

When a painful event has taken place in your own life, have you ever imagined yourself as a messenger or a conduit of positive, preventive information and care? Have you ever said to yourself, "I can't change the painful thing that happened, but I can be a part of swaying the direction this type of situation takes in the future. I can help to turn this terrible loss into something preventive, inspiring, or dignified for those who might otherwise face similar suffering or tragedy."

The Gift of Reviving Your Creativity and Commitment

Your world can be turned upside down by the loss of a job, the cancellation of a creative project, a frustrating rejection from someone in power who is afraid to take a risk, or some other type of painful setback in your work life. One moment you think you have a good chance and things were going well. But then suddenly the rug gets pulled from under your feet, and you might find yourself questioning your talent, your choices, your future security, or your trust in those who let you down.

After a painful loss (especially if weeks or months go by before a new positive opportunity emerges), your mind may be bombarded with harsh, self-critical thoughts or agitated feelings of "Why bother?" or "What's the point in trying and getting nowhere?" or "Who was I kidding? I don't have what it takes to compete at this level." At moments like this, you probably can't see that something might be happening deep inside you that will be extremely helpful in the long run. You probably aren't in the mood to say to yourself, "Gam zu l'tovah. Even this could possibly be for good."

Yet what if you were able, for even a brief moment, to look at your situation from a higher perspective or from the deep inner place where you can sense a connection to your soul, intuition, or the still, small voice within.[14] What if you could see that your heart and mind are gradually being opened by your painful situation?

One of my counseling clients is a woman named Tanya, who lost her job because her employer was going through a financial cutback. A divorced mother of two children who had gotten mostly rave reviews each year for how hard she worked, Tanya was shocked the day she got called in and downsized by a brash corporate vice president who was ten years younger (and far less intelligent) than she was. She was also terrified and somewhat depressed at the idea that it might take several months or years to find a new job in her field.

But in counseling, something wonderful happened. After several sessions of discussing her anger and feelings of loss caused by her abrupt removal from a company she had helped to build into an industry powerhouse, Tanya began to explore a radical idea: "Now that this has happened to me, what am I going to do about it to bring goodness to my family, my work life, and my own sense of growth and discovery."

I knew that she was not a very spiritual person and would probably not enjoy hearing the story of Rabbi Nachum or the phrase "Gam zu l'tovah. Even this could possibly be for good." So I didn't mention it. We talked instead about the same theme in words that made sense to Tanya—that this frustrating and unfair job loss was going to be a test of whether she was going to shut down and give up, or find some way to turn it in a positive direction.

Over the next several weeks, Tanya began to brainstorm with several of her friends, colleagues, and advisors about how to turn her skills and experiences into a positive benefit for another company that could use her services. But despite her renewed efforts, she got several unpleasant rejections and a few frustrating near-misses.

Then one morning, while we were talking about her two children and how much she enjoyed helping them express their creativity, Tanya suddenly got tears in her eyes and said, "I wish when I was their age there had been someone to help me not only learn how to do well in school and be smart, but also how to be part of a group and develop the social skills to succeed in competitive and stressful work situations."

I looked at her and asked, "Are you willing to explore these issues now, or do you feel it's too late to learn the social skills and subtle strategies that make one person successful in the work world and leave another person out in the cold?"

She took a moment and then admitted, "All my life, I've felt like a fish out of water, and I've been faking it to get by. If I could learn how to be more effective in the social and informal aspects of my career, it would make a huge difference."

That was the breakthrough moment, and over the next several months, Tanya made huge progress in both our counseling sessions and a few additional workshops she attended to discover what she had been doing wrong in social and stressful office situations that had alienated people or gotten in the way of her success at work. It was painful at times to look at herself with complete honesty. But she was courageous and did a terrific job of improving how she came across in job interviews, dealt with conflict and disagreements, and managed her own stress levels and sense of impatience.

After several months, a fascinating thing happened. One of Tanya's friends from a company she had worked at many years previously called to ask for advice about a pressing problem. During their phone call, Tanya found out about a job opportunity that turned out to be an excellent next step in her career. Not only did she get the job, but she also began to practice the improved social skills and stress management techniques we had been working on.

During her final counseling session, Tanya asked me a vulnerable question, "When I first came in for therapy and had just gotten fired, did you think of me as damaged goods?"

I took a moment and then answered honestly, "From what I

saw in our initial session and what you told me about your work experiences, I had the sense that you are an amazingly intelligent and hard-driving person who was a bit clueless about the subtle and informal social glue that connects people at work and makes them support one another on a personal level during tough times. I wasn't sure if you were going to be willing to work on those issues. But I was happy to find out that you were open to growing in that area and were definitely able to make huge improvements that will be with you for the rest of your life.

"Were you damaged goods when you first came in for counseling? No. Were you human and vulnerable? Yes. Were you willing to do the hard work to improve your life? Definitely yes."

Like many people who lose their job or have projects rejected, Tanya could have stayed stuck in her old, slightly self-defeating patterns of behavior. But instead she took the painful aftermath of getting fired and turned it into a heart-opening opportunity to become a person who was far more savvy about aspects of work that had not been easy for her in the past.

Think about your own response to various setbacks, rejections, and obstacles in your work life. What gift might these painful situations be opening you up to discover? What habits or behaviors might you now be willing to change or improve, even though you were hoping to avoid confronting these awkward parts of yourself? What kind of support, counseling, or skill building would you need to turn a painful career setback or roadblock into a source of blessings, expanded insights, and positive growth?

I don't wish for any of us to have financial distress or painful rejections. Yet I've found in my own life and those of my clients that it sometimes takes an extremely upsetting loss to shake off the layers of self-deception and complacency that keep us stuck in old habits and hold us back from attaining our full potential. Please make sure, if something happens in your work life that shows you that you are not living up to the gifts you've been given, that you take this painful situation and turn *even this* into something positive.

The Gift of Discovering That Someone Truly Cares

There is one more result that many people seem to realize from using "Gam zu l'tovah. Even this could possibly be for the good." I can't guarantee that it will work for you, but I hope you will keep your eyes open for this positive outcome to reveal itself.

When we experience an upsetting situation or a painful loss, we often tend to notice many things that are going badly and many that we wish were different. But an additional thing to look for consciously is whether one person (or maybe even more than one) shows goodness, caring, or creativity during this period of your life. It might a previously distant acquaintance or colleague who unexpectedly becomes a reliable and genuine friend as a result of deep conversations and shared humanity during a crisis. Or it might a family member, near or far, in whom the current crisis brings out the best and helps you rediscover your mutual bond. Or it might be a brief treasured moment of caring and loving-kindness from someone you barely know or with whom you have little else in common but will now always remember tenderly.

Judaism urges us repeatedly to look not just at the physical and material results in the world of externals, but to keep our eyes focused on how certain hearts are opened and certain souls express themselves with grace or goodness during life's painful struggles. Even when we suffer terrible losses, there is the possibility of a precious moment of goodness and loving-kindness between two souls that reminds us of what really matters in life.

In fact, if you read the spiritual writings of Martin Buber, who was both a psychologist and a scholar of Hasidism, he describes the holy connection between two human souls as the place where the Eternal One definitely exists. When a crisis or tragedy brings out the best in us and others, gives us a deeper friendship with someone, or allows us to appreciate a particular loved one more than ever, those are the moments when we begin to see a clear illustration of what is meant by "even this could possibly be for the good."

For example, several years ago my wife and I were trying to

start a family. We were hopeful about having children, but then we discovered we were both carriers of a rare recessive gene called Tay-Sachs, which could result in our pregnancies not being viable (a Tay-Sachs baby does not have the ability to digest food, so the newborn dies a painful death with no hope of surviving). We were told that each time we got pregnant there was a one-in-four chance that the baby would die—if both of us happened to give the gene to the fetus—and a three-in-four chance that the baby would be healthy—if either of us happened to give at least one dominant non–Tay-Sachs gene to the fetus.

We were extremely happy several months later when we discovered we were pregnant. But then we were devastated a few months after that when lab tests told us the baby wouldn't survive because it had two recessive Tay-Sachs genes. We cried, we grieved, and we wondered if we would ever be able to start a family.

Two years later, we got pregnant again. But during the next round of lab tests, we found that the one-in-four tragic outcome had occurred once more. This second child would also not be able to live beyond a few painful months or years. Losing that second child definitely knocked me to my core. It felt almost as painful as when I was fourteen years old and my beloved mother died of cancer.

For several months, Linda and I were unsure of what to do next. It took several more years of expensive and frustrating medical procedures before we were finally told by three different doctors that we would probably not be able to get pregnant a third time.

During those exhausting years of hoping for the best and getting clobbered by the worst over and over, there were a few friends, colleagues, relatives, and health practitioners who said or did some extremely insensitive and hurtful things. It's amazing how certain people with lots of formal education can still blurt out the dumbest things during a time of great sadness.

But I'm glad to report that there were also a few outstanding people who proved to be genuinely compassionate and have been a part of our lives ever since. These open-hearted individuals offered us much-needed emotional support and a willingness to listen without trying to rush or dismiss the pain we were going through. Even now, after many years, whenever I talk to or see these particular people face-to-face, I still feel enormous gratitude for the true loving-kindness they showed us during such a trying series of events.

Has there ever been someone in your own life who inspired you with his or her willingness to be of service during an especially stressful time? Or who became a much closer and more reliable part of your life because of the way he or she came through for you during a crisis. It's fascinating how the people who truly mean the most to us over an entire lifetime are often those whose hearts were open to us during our toughest challenges.

Please take a moment to bring to mind anyone who has done an excellent job of being a reliable friend or a supportive ally to you during a tough crisis. For example, maybe you and this person each got mistreated or fired by the same toxic boss, yet your friendship was strengthened and deepened by that traumatic experience. Or maybe you were both raising children at the same time and became allies by helping one another. Or possibly this person was kind or supportive when you were going through a messy divorce or breakup. Or perhaps this person was helpful and resourceful when you had a financial or medical crisis.

At the moment when the crisis is happening, it's hard to imagine that something as profound and wonderful as a lifelong friend or ally will be part of the outcome. Yet it often takes a painful crisis to find out who you can count on over the long haul. I hope that the silent words "Gam zu l'tovah. Even this could possibly be for the good" will help each of us to breathe in and appreciate the love and support we've received and that we might otherwise take for granted.

STAYING OPEN EVEN WHEN IT'S PAINFUL

I will end this chapter with one more crucial detail from those painful Tay-Sachs pregnancies. My hope is that this detail will help you whenever you are going through a painful series of set-backs and there is no relief in sight.

As I mentioned, my wife and I experienced one disappointment and setback after another over several years. Each time the phone would ring with another piece of bad news, and I had no idea when it would stop or if there would ever be an outcome that remotely resembled "even this could possibly be for the good."

You may have had times in your own life when bad news just kept coming. During those bleak episodes, there were likely moments when you felt like giving up.

Yet during those many months and years of receiving bad news, every few days, I would sit quietly in my living room as the sun was coming up or during a ten-minute break at my office and say to myself, "Gam zu l'tovah. Even this could possibly be for the good." Some days it felt empty and pointless. But on other days it gave me a crucial boost of energy to stay open and hopeful. It was like I was priming the pump inside my psyche to not give up and to remain willing to follow through on whatever God or life was guiding me to learn and do next.

To be honest, I had no clear-cut idea of what positive outcome might emerge. Week after week and month after month, there were additional referrals to specialists and more medical tests and procedures that kept raising our hopes, only to eventually be told that we were not going to able to conceive a healthy child. So it became a matter of faith to sit quietly and breathe calmly as I said, "Please God, may even this be for the good. Please keep my heart open and my eyes open for the right next steps on this journey."

Then a strange thing happened. Linda and I were taking a walk together one Sunday afternoon beside the ocean waves, and we began to discuss the possibility of no longer trying to get pregnant. For the first time, we admitted to each other that we were ready to let go completely of what wasn't happening successfully for us. Instead, we were going to start exploring the possibility of adoption.

It took a few more years and several twists and turns, but we were fortunate enough to be able to adopt our son, Steven, who has grown into a fascinating and compassionate human being. Learning each day how to do a better job of being his dad has been one of the most wonderful experiences of my life.

But I also realize in hindsight that it took a lot of sadness and huge disappointments to open us up to the idea of becoming adoptive parents. If it were not for those painful six years of two Tay-Sachs pregnancies, dozens of medical procedures, and deep grieving, I wonder if we could have opened our hearts enough to take this complicated step.

Like many other individuals, I had to learn firsthand that there is something thought-provoking and empowering about saying, "Gam zu l'tovah. Even this could possibly be for the good." Even during the most distressing times of uncertainty, when there was no indication that there would ever be a positive outcome, these words kept me open, flexible, and healthy.

I realize I was very fortunate that a joyful result did emerge after those six years of disappointment. I've found that there are no guarantees of what will happen from saying this phrase and no assurances that it will quickly break a string of bad news and frustrations that are beyond my control.

To be completely honest, I don't know exactly how God and the world operate. (In fact, I barely understand how my cell phone works.) Yet I hope that for the rest of my life—and if you so desire, for the rest of yours as well—there will be unexplainable moments of mystery and awe when I say silently, "Gam zu l'tovah. Even this could possibly be for good," and it can open up my eyes and heart to positive steps toward what is ultimately healing. Especially when we are close to giving up or numbing out, these words can keep us curious and strong as we continue to pursue our most cherished goals, values, and visions.

Please test out this phrase for yourself to see if it helps you to keep your compassion, creativity, and persistence open and alive, so you can respond well to your most distressing moments. In each of our worlds, there are likely to be some highly painful losses and deep frustrations. Yet if we are open to the possibility of something good emerging from these tough times, it may just give us the crucial boost of energy we need to find a positive gift we would otherwise miss.

7

Finding the Quiet, Peaceful Place beneath the Agitation

WHAT IF YOU'VE TRIED one or more of the techniques in this book and you're still feeling shut down or agitated? For many highly intelligent and busy people, it's not easy or automatic to meditate and relax. Please don't feel you are the only one who is having difficulty, especially if you are someone with an active mind or a frequent sense of inner edginess to contend with on stressful days.

For instance, one of my close friends told me something insightful a few months ago: "All my life, I knew that I had something like a high-rev motor inside me with lots of insecurities, antsiness, and impatience. But what I didn't know is that most of the people walking around pretending to be calm and composed are also carrying a lot of insecurities, antsiness, and impatience. So now when I close my eyes to meditate or relax, I accept the fact that I often have several layers of agitation to sift through before I reach the quiet place."

What about you? Do you ever feel like there is a motor revving inside you? Do you sometimes feel a great deal of edginess and inner agitation running through you, especially when you're over-loaded or when your plans get interrupted by all sorts of delays and distractions?

As a therapist who has had private, one-on-one conversations with thousands of clients about what really goes on inside them on a stressful day, I can assure you that even the most seemingly calm, spiritual, or composed person also has a significant amount of fog-giness or distractibility. It comes with being human. If you told me that you or anyone else never has any inner agitation, I'd probably smile and ask, "And does this person have a pulse?"

Yet for some reason, most people feel slightly ashamed of the fact that they are sometimes anxious or impatient. Or they feel defective for being a bit edgy or antsy at times. It's as though we've all been trained for years to watch the bland, emotionless news-casters on television, who barely blink as they describe horrific human tragedies, and wonder, "Why am I so keyed up while these well-dressed news icons are so flawless and unflappable?" (Never mind the fact that they all have makeup artists and hair stylists who come to the set every few minutes to make sure you never see them sweat or have a hair out of place.)

HONORING THE REASONS
FOR INNER AGITATION

Rather than feeling ashamed or self-critical for being human and contending with some internal edginess each day, what if you stopped and took a moment to explore what causes this frequent feeling of restlessness? In this chapter, I will offer a specific solu-tion that you can use whenever your inner agitation blocks your ability to meditate, relax, or enjoy your life. Gradually over time, this easy-to-use, energy-transforming technique can significantly lessen the amount and severity of your tension (even if it can't make it disappear 100 percent).

Since we human beings will always have at least some impa-tience and edginess on busy or complicated days, we might as well get to know this aspect of ourselves a little better. The following sections describe three different causes of those feelings and ways to begin managing them more successfully. See which of these descriptions sound most like you or someone you care about.

The Inner Agitation That Comes from Our Physiology

Many good people are born with a lot of impulsive energy and distractibility. For some, it's noticeable enough to be officially labeled attention deficit disorder[1] or unofficially referred to as having "ants in their pants." While many people feel embarrassed about being called anxious or easily diverted, this trait can actually be an important survival skill and creative advantage in certain situations. Often the first person to escape successfully from an oppressive nation, a toxic organization, or an abusive family situation is the one who is labeled impulsive, while the less impulsive individuals sometimes stay too long, rationalize too much, and lose the chance to find freedom.

In addition, if you study the life histories of the most highly creative and innovative people in science, the arts, social change movements, business, and many other fields, you will find that many of these remarkable individuals were accused at some point of being too impulsive or distractible. But in fact their bursts of energy and high-rev motors were among the key factors contributing to their innovative breakthroughs. For more information and techniques on how to turn attention deficit disorder or frequent distractibility into a positive attribute rather than a negative aspect of your life, please consider reading the helpful books *Delivered from Distraction* by Edward Hallowell and also *Superparenting for ADD* by Edward Hallowell and Peter Jensen.

Many individuals who don't have ADD also get keyed up when they've had too much caffeine; when their blood sugar levels are off; or when they habitually use nicotine, alcohol, and other substances that leave them jumpy and needing another dose to "take the edge off." Learning when and how much to indulge in various substances becomes a lifelong challenge for many people who come home each night with a high-rev motor that doesn't quiet down easily.

Still other men and women have an underlying physiological anxiousness or a feeling of frequent impatience that most likely results from a medical condition, a side effect of a prescription drug, a substantial increase in adolescent hormones, an occasional biochemical imbalance, complications of menopause, or some other chemical factor in the nerve endings or bloodstream that causes you to feel "like crawling out of your skin" every so often. On some days the chemical moodiness you experience in spurts of impatience or quick flashes of irritation may be quite frustrating to handle. Finding the right specialists and the most effective pharmaceutical or nonpharmaceutical approach for managing these internal chemical fluctuations can become a lifelong project that needs to be rechecked and readjusted at various ages—and especially during stressful months and years. I urge you to keep exploring your best options with trusted professionals until you find the approach that works best for your particular type of body and mind.

Unfortunately, if any of the conditions and behaviors listed here are the underlying cause of your edginess, you may be bombarding yourself with thoughts like "There's something wrong with me," "I hope no one finds out I'm like this," or "I wish I weren't this way." But, in truth, you are one of millions of decent, intelligent people who—through no fault of their own—have a complicated set of nerve endings and blood chemistries that they need to learn how to manage successfully. Rather than judging yourself or trying to hide from the recurring ups and downs you experience on a daily basis, what if you were to treat these symptoms with compassion, and the best support and guidance you can find? So that eventually you will find it easier to relax, meditate, or enjoy quiet moments.

The Inner Agitation That Comes from Difficult Life Experiences

A second reason why so many of us have to deal with a lot of inner agitation or feelings of edginess on a daily basis is because of some painful or upsetting event from the past that we've never fully processed and released. It might be a specific loss, setback, trauma, or painful memory. Or it might be a lingering aftereffect of feeling trapped for years in a household or neighborhood where there was a lot of emotional volatility, physical violence, harsh criticism, unrealistic expectations, or confusing mixed messages. Or it might be a result of feeling like an isolated outsider in social situations, school settings, religious settings, or workplaces where no matter what you said or did, you were treated like you didn't really belong.

Once again, you have two choices with regard to these traumas and painful life experiences. You can choose to view yourself as a shameful and defective disappointment. Or you can begin the process of discovering (with a counselor, coach, friend, adviser, spiritual mentor, or private journal) the real reasons why these events happened and how to heal from them.

The Inner Agitation That Comes from Overcompensating for Your Imperfections

Finally, the third reason why many people walk around with a lot of edginess is that they are secretly trying to prove their self-worth. People often become extremely demanding of themselves in order to overcompensate for some imperfection or mistake for which they haven't fully forgiven themselves. In many cases, we become enormously demanding of others (feeling impatient or judgmental toward our coworkers, our kids, our friends, our leaders, or our public figures), because we are secretly upset about the setbacks or unrealized dreams in our own lives.

If you ever notice yourself becoming a bit rigid, self-righteous, demanding, gossipy, or unforgiving toward yourself or others, you may benefit by asking yourself, "Why am I feeling so judgmental and agitated inside right now? What imperfection of mine am I trying to run away from? What impossible standard am I trying to apply to myself or others to make up for what I haven't fully accepted about how life works?"

FINDING A PLACE UNDERNEATH THE AGITATION

Now we come to something very exciting and helpful. In Jewish spirituality, there is a beautiful phrase that I've often found can take you from a place of agitation to a deeper place where there is peace and relief from the various types of antsiness and impatience that most of us experience on stressful days.

There is clear documentation in the Talmud (the legal and practical interpretations of how to live a life of goodness) that this uplifting meditation phrase was recited daily at least two thousand years ago.[2] It has been spoken softly, reflected upon silently, or sung aloud as a centering technique through the highest highs and the lowest lows of human history ever since.

Essentially this brief meditation phrase is a way of letting go of your attachment to the agitation you feel in your nerves, muscles, and thoughts. It allows you instead to connect with a deeper and less stressed you that is much purer than the surface mind-body shell you live within. This inspirational phrase is a quick and effective way to break free of physicality and glimpse the level of the soul or the deep inner calmness that exists within each of us (even when we are too busy to notice it).

Here are the words of this spiritual phrase (in Hebrew and in English):

Elohai, n'shamah shenatata bi, t'horah hi. My God, the soul that You have placed within me is a pure one!

If for any reason you are not comfortable with saying "My God" as the source of how your soul is placed within your body and renewed each day, you can translate *Elohai* as "mysterious One," "infinite Source of all that exists," or "endless flow of creative energy."

In the fuller version that Jews throughout history have sung or recited each morning, the meditation is expanded:

> My God, the soul that You have placed in me is a pure one!
> You have created and formed it,
> breathed it into me,
> and within me You sustain it . . .
> So long as I have breath, therefore,
> I will give thanks to You.

The meditation (either the single sentence or the entire paragraph) should be recited slowly, with appreciation for each word and concept. In most traditional prayer books and congregations, an additional phrase is recited after the ellipsis that says, "and eventually You will take it from me, and restore it to me in Time to Come." If you were raised in a family or a congregation that said, "Jews don't believe in the afterlife," you may want to think again. There are many Jewish teachings and beliefs about how the soul continues beyond death. [3]

Notice for a moment what this complete meditation says about who you really are. It declares that deep underneath your slightly imperfect body, your emotional turmoil, and your impatient thoughts there is a protected place inside you that is pure. Genuinely pure. Not defective. Not ashamed. Not alone and lonely. Not cut off from the Source. Not limited by this one particular lifetime.

If you were taught as a child (by your parents or by the schools and culture you grew up in) that human beings are basically evil, fallen, narrow, or adrift in this world, then certainly this Jewish meditation is going to challenge what you were taught. It says that our surface-level behaviors may sometimes be cautious, sneaky, distracted, or lacking in follow-through, or our bodies may be clumsy or a bit out of shape. But deep inside there is a core essence—a unique and exquisite soul—that is pure and connects daily to a flowing power source that seems to be infinite and extremely positive.

For a quick moment, let's dig deeper to find out what this mystical paragraph is describing about how you truly function in this universe. The word *n'shamah* means "soul" or "breath." In this prayer/meditation, you are being asked to remember the moment you were born, when a powerful breath or life force from an infinite Source of energy became your first expansive inhalation and exhalation. If you have ever watched the relaxed breathing of a sleeping infant or sensed the soul or essence of a newborn child and seen just how pure and open it is, you may have had a glimpse into what happens in this particular meditation—you open a portal, a gateway to that pure and holy part of yourself.

Certainly you've taken on many layers of agitation, defenses, and distractions since your first breath. But in this potentially liberating meditation, you may be able to reexperience the excitement, gratitude, and joy of being given the gift of life. Like a child opening his or her eyes for the first time or taking in that first healthy breath of fresh air, you might feel a sense of wonderment at connecting with your deepest core essence.

In addition, this prayer/meditation points out the fact that each day we breathe anew. Here's what it says in practical terms: Each night when we close our eyes and surrender to sleep, we essentially let go of control and consciousness. This requires a certain amount of trust that "You [the ever-flowing life force of the universe] will sustain it [the precious soul] within me."

We then start each day with a new breath and a renewed sense of purpose and possibilities. According to Judaism, our individual soul/breath/n'shamah is recharged one day at a time by an infinite Soul/Breath/Source that surrounds and is deep within us. Even if yesterday was extremely stressful and disturbing, when you say this prayer/meditation you open up to the reality that your pure soul, your exquisite core essence, is still intact and intimately connected once again to its Ultimate Source.

UNDERSTANDING THE SCIENTIFIC ASPECTS
OF THIS MEDITATION

From a scientific perspective, there's a possible connection between your individual soul/breath/essence and the invisible Soul/Breath/Ultimate Essence that can be understood if you think about your physical pulse and the actual fluids in your digestive system. (Please note that some scientists and physicians strongly endorse this theory, while others disagree with it.)

Right now, as you are reading this paragraph, you have blood pulsing through you (at least I hope you do), and there are all sorts of fluids in your stomach. Your pulse beats consistently, and your stomach fluids move a little bit every minute, even when you're unaware of them or are stressed out and focused on other things.

What you might not have realized is that your pulse and your stomach fluids are impacted constantly by all sorts of subtle energy fields. Like the ever-flowing ocean tides that rise and fall predictably according to the cycles of the moon, your pulse rate and your stomach juices are also constantly pulled to varying degrees by the lunar gravitational force. (Most women are somewhat aware of the pull of the moon on their internal fluids because of their monthly cycles, but men are pulled too).[4]

According to some scientists and physicians, your pulse and your stomach fluids are also affected by the rays of the sun, electro-magnetic fields, and the light waves all around you. That's why many people feel a bit different when they're in a room with fluorescent lights instead of outdoors with natural light from the sun.[5]

Additional studies suggest that your internal bodily functions are sensitive to the sound waves around you. Just ask anyone what happens to their pulse, internal organs, and digestive muscles when they're in a room filled with loud music; a room with a single, irritatingly repetitive noise; and a room that is completely still.

Since most of us have been raised in a society that values individuality, self-reliance, and compartmentalization of different aspects of life, you may feel that you are essentially isolated and cut off from everything around you. But some scientists and most body experts say that your physical energy and moods are influenced to some extent by the moon, sun, light waves, and sound waves that surround you and connect you with hard-to-see forces, causing subtle reactions inside you.

Now let's apply this notion of interconnectedness to your individual soul/breath/essence and how it relates to the infinite but hard-to-see Soul/Breath/Essence. Specifically, when you say the words of the meditation phrase, "Elohai, n'shamah shenatata bi, t'horah hi. My God, the soul You placed within me is a pure one," you can experience a profound and truer version of who you really are—a pure soul, a ray of energy living in a material body and connected to a strong Source; this Source infused you with vitality and insights when you were first born and now infuses new life and subtle guidance into you each day.

Because your individual essence is connected to a universal Essence, it is continually being revived and renewed. Even on a stressful day, when your nerves are jumbled and your thoughts are edgy, there is still a pure essence or soul deep inside you that draws strength from a pulsing universal energy. In other words, just like your underlying physical pulse still does quite well even on a demanding day, your n'shamah or pure essence stays strong and vibrant even when your outer shell is feeling agitated. Taking a moment to refocus your attention and connect strongly with that exquisite soul inside you—your n'shamah—may free you from anxiety and take you instead to a peaceful place. With repeated practice, this place can gradually begin to radiate throughout your entire being each time you say these words.

PUTTING THIS INTO PRACTICE

Let's see what happens if you take a deep breath in and out as you say with sincerity,

Elohai, n'shamah shenatata bi, t'horah hi.
My God (or Source of all that exists),

The soul that you have placed in me is a pure one!
You have created and formed it,
breathed it into me,
and within me You sustain it . . .
So long as I have breath, therefore,
I will thank You.

As you repeat this meditation two or three times, imagine that you are traveling deep inside your being to a place that is beyond your physical limitations, beyond your moods and emotions, beyond your thoughts and nerve endings. Imagine for a few seconds that you are able to connect with your pure essence, the soul deep inside you.

As you breathe calmly, take a minute to connect with your genuine internal home—the protected place where your soul exists. In that deep and insightful place, you are no longer pressured, rushed, or inadequate. As you spend a few relaxing moments dwelling in that comfortable place, you are no longer anxious or conflicted. You are genuinely home, and there is a sense of peace and wholeness.

While everyone who tries this meditation phrase has slightly different results, I have found that, sooner or later, many people who say these words sincerely and calmly over a period of days, weeks, or months do catch a glimpse of what it's like to be at peace, to be at one with their own soul and with the awesome Soul of the universe.

UNSURE OF THE WORD SOUL?

It's not easy for many men and women to believe they have a soul or an invisible essence. For example, I recently counseled a woman named Sondra who, like many of my clients, doesn't believe in the concept of a personal soul or an ultimate Soul of the universe. As I listened to her express these doubts, I was tempted for a moment to try to talk her out of her feelings. But then I took a breath and let her tell me more about her frustrations regarding the religious experiences in her upbringing that had given her so much distaste for religion and spirituality in general.

Generally when a therapy client expresses his or her discomfort with words like *soul* or *God,* I just listen and don't argue. My job as a therapist is not to tell anyone what to believe; rather, it is to understand and work with the beliefs and values the client holds dear.

So with Sondra, I asked, "What particular words or favorite methods do you use to wake up your energy each day and connect with an inspiring source of positive feelings? For instance, are you replenished by talking with supportive people, reading inspiring works, spending time in solitude and quiet, being in nature, listening to music, or doing something creative?"

Like many other creative people who have substantial doubts about various spiritual and religious beliefs, Sondra told me she often found strength and peace when she was in nature. She explained, "If I do some gardening or spend just a half hour walking in nature, I usually reconnect with that strong, intuitive part of me that I often lose touch with during a stressful week."

Based on this response, I asked her to say the meditation for finding a peaceful place deep inside by using words that matched her own experience of being reenergized by gardening and taking walks outdoors. As a result, whenever she felt depleted, distracted, or insecure, Sondra began to say the following words to herself (which she repeated three times so they would reach deep inside her being):

Life force that is found in nature, the energy that you give me is pure. Creative force that I experience in nature, the energy boost that you give me is pure. Creative life force that shows up in nature, the energy boost that you give me is pure.

Even if these phrases, written by Sondra, sound substantially different from the Elohai, n'shamah prayer, the words are, in fact, nearly identical. Instead of saying, "My God," Sondra was more comfortable using "Life force," "Creative force," or "Creative life force," which are legitimate ways of addressing God in Jewish mysticism and spirituality. Instead of using the word *soul,* she felt better saying "the pure energy boost," which is somewhat similar to the Jewish notion of a pure breath that connects with your core essence or n'shamah.

Sondra began to practice saying her own customized meditation phrases for a few minutes each day, whenever she was feeling insecure, impatient, or edgy. After a few weeks, she told me, "It's surprising. When I take a deep breath and say these words a few times with a sense of sincerity and openness, especially if I visualize myself being in nature, I usually get this strong, centered feeling. For me, those are the moments when I can best experience my own inner strength. Even if I'm feeling drained by all the pressures in my career and personal life, those moments of paying attention to the pure life force of nature remind me of who I am deep inside."

As Sondra's case illustrates, it doesn't really matter what words you use, as long as they take you to that same pure place of inner peace. While some people call the center of their being a soul, or their spark of the Divine, others call it their pure essence, life force, or internal inspiration. Ironically, all of these different words are perfectly valid definitions of the Hebrew word *n'shamah.*

If you or someone you know has been blocked from using spiritual methods because of a particular word or idea that felt awkward, please take this opportunity to substitute a similar word that has no unpleasant side-effect. Just like if you are lactose intolerant and you can't drink cow's milk but you do get nourishment from soy or rice milk, please know that if you are allergic or have a negative visceral reaction to one particular spiritual or religious word, you don't need to extricate yourself completely from the many benefits of this spiritual centering method. By replacing a particular word that you don't find believable with a similar word that you do find inspiring and useful, you can definitely connect with the same internal place of strength and peacefulness.

Sadly, we live in a world where a person from religious denomination Z tends to argue with or get angry at a person from denomination Y, who calls these concepts by a different name. But since many words describe a similar process of connecting with our pure essence, let's not quibble about our differing beliefs as to how it all works. I believe there's plenty of room in this world for a variety of ways to define the same peaceful feeling of "at-one-ment." For the past thirty years I've been involved in many formal and informal dialogue groups between Jews and Christians, Jews and Muslims, religious conservatives and liberals, spiritual believers and nonbelievers. It's amazing how much we all long to connect with the hard-to-comprehend source of strength and goodness that we each describe in such diverse ways.

REMEMBERING TO CHOOSE WISELY
DURING A STRESSFUL MOMENT

What matters most is whether, during a moment of impatience or agitation, you go back to the old habit of numbing out or remember to do something different that can raise your energy and strength without any negative after-effects. It may take days, weeks, or months of practicing this particular meditation before it starts to come naturally to you in the middle of a stressful day. But if you successfully get in the habit of using it to regain your calm and reduce your level of anxiety, you will be enormously blessed.

I want to end this chapter with the story of Nolan, an interesting young man who, in his early twenties, began to discover all sorts of messy ways to deal with his frequent feelings of agitation and impatience. He grew up with a very creative mom who was anxious and a dad who would tune out his wife and kids. Nolan's father immersed himself in work during the week, watching endless sports programs on television each weekend, and having a few stiff drinks each night to numb out.

Nolan told me during his initial counseling session that he had made a decision when he was a teenager that he didn't want to be anything like his anxious mom or his shut-down dad. So he began to experiment with various mood-altering drugs that his friends told him would set him free from the limitations of his parents' narrow mind-sets.

Yet by the time he was twenty-two, he found that he was becoming more and more numb (like his dad) and also more agitated and impatient with anything that took a while to come to fruition (like his mom). He usually had trouble finishing his assignments and felt embarrassed about not yet completing the coursework for his degree. He also described how he sometimes had trouble listening patiently when a lover or friend wanted him to be fully present. He occasionally had trouble holding back his anger and impatience with bad drivers on the road or with rigid landlords and noisy neighbors in various apartment buildings.

At a relatively young age, Nolan's daily life had become a battle between the part of him that wanted to stay distracted by surfing the Internet, smoking marijuana, and eating numerous bags of chips and the part of him that wanted to be successful at achieving his career goals, building a quality relationship, and having genuine friends.

We made an enormous amount of progress in the first few weeks, helping Nolan sort out what he wanted to keep and what he wanted to discard from his parents' values and lifestyles. It turned out that he longed to include some of his mother's creative enthusiasm and some of his dad's career focus in his adult persona, even though he was sure he didn't want to replicate his mother's anxious way of overreacting to almost everything or his father's habit of tuning out anything that didn't fall within his narrow range of interests. But Nolan was worried that he would always fall short of his goals because he tended to get distracted.

So I told him that whenever he felt edgy or experienced a craving for some numbing-out activity (whether it was food, drugs, or Internet surfing), he could immediately take a deep, nourishing breath and pull out a small note card on which he had already written the following words:

Elohai, n'shamah shenatata bi, t'horah hi.
Source of all that exists, the soul that You have placed in me is
    a pure one!
You have created it and formed it,
You breathed it into me,
and within me You sustain it . . .
So long as I have breath, therefore,
I will give thanks to You.

I asked Nolan to promise to use this reminder card whenever he was about to get sidetracked from his important goals and projects. Almost like putting on a pair of sunglasses before walking out in the bright sun, he could use this meditation to protect himself from being overwhelmed or knocked off center.

A few weeks later, I heard back from Nolan, who told me, "Having an actual note card in my hand to keep me focused has definitely helped. When I breathe in deeply and pull that card out of my wallet, I make sure to read it slowly three times. The first time I still have a pretty strong craving for something distracting—some way of tuning out the feelings. The second time I start to feel as though I'm traveling deep inside to reach the pure place where I can remember that I have a good soul that is not always edgy or agitated. By the third time I read the card, I often begin to feel kind of peaceful, as if I've found a quiet, strong place inside me where I don't need to numb out."

As a result of doing this meditation technique, Nolan began to improve significantly at following through on his goals and not getting diverted. He eventually finished the requirements for his degree and began to work for a creative organization that loved his high-energy approach to life. He became a lot less anxious and a lot more patient and thoughtful in his personal relationships. He eventually stopped using street drugs and started training for a long-distance walk-a-thon charity event. He even cut back on his Internet surfing, which freed up a lot of time for pursuing his long-delayed goals.

If you or someone you know have found it difficult to remember to use your most effective meditation and focusing techniques when you truly need them, you may find it helpful to put this inspiring meditation paragraph on a small note card that you can keep handy for use in an agitated moment. It's like a cognitive-spiritual Get Out of Jail Free card that helps you to remember who you truly are and what you are on earth to do.

8

Seeing New Possibilities in Each Moment

SOMETIMES WHAT MAKES A DAY especially stressful is when you feel stuck doing the same things over and over. Maybe it's your daily commute that has irritating moments almost every time. Or your daily struggle to get one of your children up, dressed, and ready to go. Or your frequent phone calls from a family member, friend, colleague, boss, or client who wants more from you than you feel able to give right now. Or your daily scheduling dilemma to find enough time for a personal creative project or your favorite hobby.

In 1993, there was an unusual and highly praised film called *Groundhog Day,* starring Bill Murray and Andie MacDowell, in which the main character was stuck in a repetitive time loop. Each day began with the same whiny Sonny and Cher song on the clock-radio. No twenty-four-hour period really changed anything, because the next day started over again with the exact same problems and frustrations.

The main character began to feel increasingly despondent and upset, because no matter what he did each day, he was still trapped in the same repetitive loop with no forward momentum. I won't give away the positive and inspiring ending in case you have never seen the film, but I will point out that for many millions of good and decent individuals, each new day feels almost as repetitive, stuck, and stressful as the scenes in this classic film.

So let me ask you a tough question: in your own life (or that of someone you care about), is there a repetitive loop that gets on your nerves? Is there a recurring dilemma or frustrating situation that causes you to feel trapped or stressed every so often? Do you experience a sense of irritation sometimes because day after day certain difficult things don't seem to get better?

CREATING A SHIFT IN YOUR CONSCIOUSNESS

Fortunately, there is a highly effective remedy for overcoming the "same old, same old" blahs. It can shift your consciousness from feeling trapped in a rut and open you up to a more alive and satisfying daily experience of constant discovery, curiosity, newness, and forward momentum.

I've saved this particular remedy for the last chapter of this book because it is the meditation phrase I tend to use most often in my own life, and I'm hoping it will be the one you remember most clearly when you finish reading and get back to your daily activities. I tend to say it slowly and carefully to myself nearly each time I start a new activity or when I get in my car, and I try to remember to say it whenever something anxiety-producing or challenging is about to happen on a busy or stressful day.

This phrase has helped numerous women and men I have counseled, who use it as part of their daily stress management. In Hebrew, it is called the *Shehecheyanu,* which in English means to stop in the middle of a busy life and realize that you are doing something important, unique, and wonderful for the very first time.

Most religious and slightly religious Jews know this phrase as something they say at holidays, baby namings, major celebrations, and big events to acknowledge and appreciate a special day. Many other Jews say it whenever they are about to experience any positive or unique experience, such as eating a piece of fresh fruit when it is first in season, receiving a much-appreciated gift, seeing a beloved person they haven't seen for a while, moving into a new home, or celebrating a new chapter in their life.[1]

In addition, many Jewish meditation teachers, mystics, and scholars recommend using this phrase as a frequent mindfulness wake-up call to retrain your brain to live in a genuine state of curiosity, creativity, alertness, and joy. Instead of taking each moment for granted or rushing from stressful event to stressful event, this centering phrase gives you a chance to stop briefly; breathe deeply; and appreciate the new possibilities for growth, improvement, and joy that exist even on a day that seems like every other day. It opens you up to the remarkable possibility that the next moment of your life may be more compassionate, centered, healthy, and mindful than the previous times when you were in a similar situation.

In some ways, the Hebrew and English Shehecheyanu phrase is a lot like the concept of "beginner's mind" in Zen Buddhism, where each moment is a journey in itself that begins with an open, curious, nondogmatic, flexible mind.[2] According to some Buddhist teachers, by allowing yourself to "not know" and instead to be curious, compassionate, and open, you are able to experience the newness and enormous possibilities in every single moment. You are no longer trapped in a *Groundhog Day* repetitive loop with no future. Rather, you are able to see the opportunity to be more mindful and compassionate that can be found in every moment.

The traditional Hebrew phrase that has been recited at moments of joy, newness, and celebration for thousands of years is as follows:

Baruch Atah, Adonai Eloheinu, Melech haolam, shehecheyanu v'kiy'manu v'higianu laz'man hazeh.

This can be translated as any one of the following:

Blessed are You, Eternal One, Ruler of the Universe, who has kept us alive and sustained us and enabled us to reach this unique moment.

Blessed are You, Eternal One, Ruler of the Universe, who has kept us in life and sustained us and helped us to reach this season.

Blessed are You, Eternal One, Ruler of the Universe, who keeps us vibrant and sustains us and helps us experience this moment of joy.

For some of my counseling clients, a shorter and more personalized phrase is most effective. Here are a few of the phrases they have come up with on their own and used as a meditative wake-up call on busy days:

Thank you, Infinite Source, for giving us life and keeping us strong and guiding us to reach this moment for good.

Blessed is the indescribable One that is the Ultimate Source of our energy and that directs us to this unique moment of possibilities right now.

I am thankful to the One that brought me to this moment so that I can experience whatever happens next with joy and wisdom and love.

I appreciate the Source of all that exists that has given me life and kept me going and allowed me to reach this unique moment of endless possibilities.

I bless and thank the unknowable Presence that gave me life, keeps me going each day, and allows me to experience this next moment of goodness.

As you think about your own way of speaking, what words might you choose to shift your mind from seeing a stressful moment as the same old thing and beginning to see it as a unique new moment that is rich in possibilities? What particular phrase might allow you to open your mind and heart to the fact that you are a cocreator of what happens next—that you can make a difference in whether the next moment of your life tilts toward boredom, distance, and dread or moves toward creativity, warmth, and goodness?

CONNECTING WITH POSITIVE INSIGHTS

One of the benefits of saying the Shehecheyanu meditation phrase in the middle of a stressful day is that it encourages your mind to locate and connect with positive insights and innovations, even when you are experiencing interruptions, delays, setbacks, or difficult people. For example, here's what happened to one of my counseling clients, a talented but struggling writer named Marta:

I first met Marta when she attended one of my workshops, then she made an appointment for individual counseling. Smart, humorous, and sensitive, she had been struggling for several years to make a living as a writer. One of her excellent scripts had gotten some nibbles from several producers and viable companies, but it never quite reached the level of earning Marta any money. One of her books was published by a small publisher, but it was overshadowed in the marketplace because a similar book by a well-known author got nearly all the media attention. Marta had begun to write for several blogs and websites, for which she admits, "If I add up all the money I've made from these online sites, it's almost enough to buy a new refrigerator—but not quite."

In counseling, we discovered that Marta was losing her sense of hope and had begun to experience writer's block because "each new writing project feels as if it's my last desperate chance to become successful. Unfortunately, that pressure is making my brain feel all twisted up and blocked sometimes."

During her first few weeks of therapy, we made progress on several issues, especially her frustrating relationship with her highly critical parents and her superattractive, younger sister, Elise, who was having a much easier ride on life's rollercoaster. According to Marta, "Elise always seems to make things happen. She completed her law degree and got recruited by a prestigious firm. She found a great guy to marry. She even popped out two kids and hired a nanny to raise them. She also bought a house that looks like it was in last month's *Architectural Digest*. It's not easy being her less-than-successful, never-married, sagging older sister."

Instead of spending her life feeling one down compared to her sister or feeling less than sufficient compared to her parents' constant suggestions and expectations, something began to change for Marta after a few weeks of practicing this particular meditation phrase. I began to see that she was making significant progress in several challenging areas each week.

Specifically, I found that Marta was becoming far more productive and creative by saying the Shehecheyanu meditation phrase once or twice every day when she was about to do something difficult or complicated. Physically and emotionally, she seemed a lot more alive and alert from using these words that essentially said to her conscious and subconscious mind, "This next moment is unique and new. It is filled with endless possibilities. Don't be afraid."

According to Marta, "Something shifted in my way of thinking when I started breathing calmly and looking at each new writing session and pitch meeting through the lens of the Shehecheyanu perspective. Instead of the sense of dread I tended to feel in the past, I would sit down in front of my computer to begin each day's session by saying, 'Thank you, Loving Presence, for making me a creative person and giving me the energy and the passion to write. Thank you for bringing me to this moment of goodness.'"

Marta discovered that this brief meditation significantly changed the way she felt about her writing and creativity. She began to write about important topics and themes that she cared about deeply. She began to create characters that were much more vivid and interesting than any she had written previously. She began to feel more confident and alive at her pitch meetings and at face-to-face sessions with producers and executives. While she still received some rejections and hesitations from what she calls the "cautious suits who make the final decisions," she managed to sell one project to an excellent actress-producer and also arranged for two solid writing assignments during the next twelve months.

As she found, "It wasn't just the ritual of saying the Shehecheyanu as a way to break out of my long-time rut of fear and dread. It was also the fact that the more I said this meditation, the stronger I felt to bring forward my most unique and meaningful ideas. In the past, I was sometimes so focused on pleasing people or trying to figure out what they might want to buy that it cramped my style. Now that I was saying a daily meditation about appreciating the gift of life and celebrating this unique new moment, I felt much freer to be more creative and genuine."

Marta also discovered that the Shehecheyanu helped her to feel more courageous and self-confident each time she was out on a date or in social situations where she was looking for a possible partner: "I still don't have a perfect body, but I noticed that I feel a lot more relaxed, comfortable, alive, and engaging when I say to myself before each date or social event, 'I am blessing the Source that gives me life, that keeps me feeling vibrant and curious, and that brings me to this new moment that has unlimited possibilities.' To be honest, that meditation phrase is a lot more empowering than what I used to say to myself—namely, 'Oh shoot, do I have to do this again. I'm just going to get rejected one more time.'"

Marta is one of many people I've counseled who found that their creative flow and courage in anxiety-producing situations were enhanced by saying the Shehecheyanu. I've seen this meditation help clients overcome their fear of public speaking, of saying yes and following through on goals and dreams they had been putting off for years, of being vulnerable and honest in a relationship, and of developing a new business or nonprofit venture.

A SCIENTIFIC PERSPECTIVE

Let's examine for a moment what happens when you set out on a new phase of your journey each day with your eyes open wider because of a meditation that says, "Thank you for sustaining us and bringing us to this unique moment for good." Does it truly make a difference if you stop first and make sure that you alert your mind to watch for new possibilities and creative opportunities that a less alert or less centered person might overlook? Is it possible for a meditation phrase or a specific set of words to make you more responsive to new possibilities and opportunities that show up occasionally than if you just went through your busy day without stopping to refocus?

For centuries many researchers and scientific theorists have examined whether a positive silent suggestion or an internal shift in perspective can improve overall creativity or the ability to see what others fail to see.[3] One of the best scientific explanations of how this works can be found in the classic book *The Structure of Scientific Revolutions* by Thomas Kuhn, which explores the intricacies of scientific research and how new ideas, inventions, and medical breakthroughs occur for certain kinds of thinkers but not for others.[4]

Kuhn was a physicist and a scholar of the history of science who taught at Harvard, the University of California at Berkeley, Princeton, and Massachusetts Institute of Technology. He spent a major portion of his life studying exactly what happens in a laboratory that causes some researchers to overlook a possible scientific breakthrough, while others are able to notice and build constructively on anomalous or divergent pieces of data. In other words, why do some people have the creative ability to see and do something positive with new possibilities, while others are stuck repeating the same things over and over, even when there are new data or new possibilities right in front of them?

In *The Structure of Scientific Revolutions,* Kuhn refers to a famous psychological study by Jerome Bruner and Leo Postman at Harvard University, in which a sizable number of human volunteers were shown ordinary playing cards that had been mixed up with a few anomalous or unusual cards like a black three of hearts. The results of the study showed that many of the volunteers said they saw what they expected to see (either they thought they saw the three of spades or the three of hearts in its usual red, but not the actual black three of hearts found in the experiment). Only a small percentage of people were able to see beyond their expectations and notice that they were seeing something new and interesting—a black three of hearts.[5] From this psychological study and several other scientific examples, Kuhn was able to establish that it takes a particular individual with a particular frame of mind that is actively looking for anomalies and unusual data to see the subtle but unique possibilities for change and newness that are all around us.

According to Kuhn, many researchers (in science and all other areas of life) can only see what they expect to see based on their past experiences and prior conclusions. He demonstrated how, when we are left to our own habits, most of us fail to see a new possibility because our minds are so entrenched in looking at things as we have in the past. Yet if you consciously do something to train yourself to keep your eyes open, you can then be the rare individual who sees what Kuhn described as a paradigm shift—a way of creatively looking at the uniqueness of what is in front of you and seeing new possibilities, combinations, and opportunities.

Kuhn wrote about numerous important breakthroughs in the sciences, medicine, and other fields that happened only because some individuals had trained themselves to intentionally stay open and not settle for the same old explanation of existing data.

Instead, these extra-alert, and extraperceptive people were usually the ones to see that a positive paradigm shift was possible.

Some people are naturally able to see what others fail to notice. Yet most of us need a little assistance to open our eyes and mind to new possibilities. We need something each day to help us see what's truly possible rather than being limited by what happened in the past. The Shehecheyanu is a quick way of saying to your conscious and subconscious mind, "You are now in a unique, new moment that has never existed before exactly like this. Be open to it. Be fully present and aware during this moment. Don't just rely on what the past tells you is going on. Recognize and be grateful that there might be a clue for improvement, growth, and unique opportunities in this upcoming moment."

A SPIRITUAL PERSPECTIVE

In most spiritual and religious traditions, there are specific prayers, meditations, and teachings to help people achieve new beginnings instead of remaining stuck in established habits and tendencies. There are two quick examples I'd like to offer to illustrate how this works. One is from my wife, and the other is from the book of Exodus in the Torah.

The first example applies if you have a few difficult relatives or occasional complicated family situations; here is a way to use the Shehecheyanu as a creative remedy. For many years, my wife, Linda, found that she felt stressed and frustrated at large family events and holiday gatherings where there were lots of ego clashes, unsolicited advice from relatives, and occasional hurtful comments. So a number of years ago, when we were driving up to a family member's house for a big gathering, she said to me, "Hey, I'm feeling stressed. How about if we say a prayer before walking in the door."

We both took a deep breath, and my wife said calmly and spontaneously, "Please God, open me up to the unexpected possibility that something good might happen in the next few hours here."

Then we said the Shehecheyanu meditation together to alert our minds that this was a new moment with unique possibilities, especially if we were willing to be less reactive and more creative in how we handled the gathering.

You may have noticed some ironic humor in the phrase "the unexpected possibility of something good." In essence, my wife was honoring the fact that there have been some difficult family encounters in the past. She was also opening her mind and heart (as well as my mind and heart) to the possibility that something good might happen at this particular gathering. It might be the chance to spend a few quality minutes with a beloved elderly family member we both enjoy enormously or a few precious minutes interacting with an adorable niece or nephew who we don't get to see very often. It might be that one or both of us was better prepared this time to use an effective escape phrase if we got cornered by one of our more toxic relatives. Or an unexpected good moment might happen in the middle of a tense family argument between two other relatives, when my wife and I would be able to look across the room at one another and signal with our eyes, "I'm with you. This too shall pass."

Ever since we first tried it out at that particular family event, we have found repeatedly that this quick Shehecheyanu and humorously ironic centering prayer ("May I be open to something unexpectedly good here") can successfully allow the possibility for something new and positive to happen. Even though many things haven't improved at our extended family gatherings, just saying the words prior to each event has made a huge difference in helping both of us be more creative, more forgiving, more compassionate, and better at drawing healthy boundaries.

It's amazing how many genuine improvements you can see if you say to your conscious and subconscious, "This is a new unique moment, and I'm looking for new data and new combinations that are possible for creating genuine steps toward progress." Try it out a few times before your next family event or some other anxiety-producing social gathering and see what happens.

The second example of how to understand the Shehecheyanu meditation from a spiritual or religious viewpoint comes from Exodus 3:14. At that point in the epic story of the Jewish people, Moses was feeling stressed and anxious, because most of the wanderers in the desert were becoming restless and dissatisfied. So he asked the Eternal One, "If the people are worried about whether You exist, and if they ask me for Your Name, what shall I tell them?"

He heard the following answer: "Ehiyeh Asher Ehiyeh," which in the King James version of the Bible is translated as "I am who I am." But if you study the Hebrew grammar carefully regarding this sentence, which is spoken in the first person singular imperfect form of *hayah* (to be), a better translation would say, "I will be what I will be," or "I am becoming what I am becoming."[6] According to numerous scholars, this implies that the Eternal One is not a fixed entity stuck in one limited form. Rather, the response to Moses's anxious question is, "I am forever changing, evolving, growing, interacting, transforming. . . . I am becoming what I am becoming." In other words, when you say the Shehecheyanu, you connect with the fact that the universe (and the Creative Source) is constantly evolving and changing. Each moment is unique and unlike any previous moment. The possibilities are endless, and the Source is also endless.

When you stop for a moment in the middle of a stressful day and say consciously, "Thank You for bringing me to this new, unique moment for good," you address not only an ever-flowing Source that urges you to be open to change and improvement, but also a compassionate Source that is open to changing and improving along with you.

As a psychologist, I realize there are many reasons why people close down their hearts and minds and why they feel so anxious and stressed about making changes and dealing with what is new and unfamiliar. But in Jewish spirituality, there is a basic underlying emphasis that life is a continuous flow, always changing and always new. You can freeze up in fear and anxiety, or you can breathe deeply and say to the Creative Source (in the paraphrased words of the Shehecheyanu), "Thank You for all the previous moments when You have kept me alive and guided me, and most of all, thank You for the unique new moment of opportunity and growth that is in front of me right now." It doesn't matter whether you are thirteen, thirty-three, or eighty-three. Saying the Shehecheyanu is a chance to open up and rejoice in the uniqueness of the present moment.

PUTTING THIS INTO PRACTICE

As you think about the still-to-be-discovered next few hours and days that you will experience soon, please take a moment to ask yourself if your heart and mind are open and curious or if you are feeling blocked and sluggish because you are expecting the same old thing that's happened in the past. Then take a deep breath and see if you can say with genuine sincerity, "I am grateful to the ever-flowing Source of Life that has kept us alive, sustained us, and brought us to this unique and new moment for discovering what's possible and what may be healing, positive, and improving. Baruch Atah, Adonai Eloheinu, Melech haolam, shehecheyanu v'kiy'manu v'higianu laz'man hazeh."

WHAT COMES NEXT?

I assume that you have now read and tried out at least one and possibly several of the methods described in this book. Please know that it might take a number of attempts before you realize the full benefits of these meditations and remedies. Don't stop trying just because it takes a while to get completely comfortable and familiar with these methods. I've found the more you use them, the more effective they become.

I've also found, in listening to many counseling clients, that there will be moments when you forget to use these remedies or when you are just too busy to give them the full attention and relaxed breathing that will make them optimally effective. I'm not expecting perfection or 100 percent compliance. But I do hope you (and your friends, colleagues, students, or family members with whom you will be sharing these teachings and techniques) will have many noticeable breakthroughs now and in the future.

As you reach the end of these eight chapters, please accept my genuine thanks that you were willing to read some (or all) of this book that I've been researching and writing for so many years. I appreciate that your life is stressful at times and that you are busy, so I'm extremely glad you are taking positive steps to improve how you deal with these stresses. My hope is that this book has significantly increased how much you are able to celebrate life; to make each day more mindful and compassionate; and to do your part in repairing this fragile world which desperately needs your ideas, caring, and creativity.

May you be blessed each day of your life with wisdom, with love, and with strength.

Acknowledgments

It has taken several villages to help me write this book. I am grateful that I grew up in Detroit one block away from my maternal grandparents, William and Pauline Rothenberg, who taught me a lot about Jewish living. I ws also fortunate to study for twelve years at Temple Israel, where I was guided by many wonderful teachers, including Helen Gilbert, Cantor Harold Orbach, and Rabbi M. Robert Syme.

At Kenyon College in Ohio, I was fortunate to study with Dr. Rowland Shepard, who taught me about Dr. Viktor Frankl and the connection between psychological counseling and Jewish spirituality. While living in New York, I was guided by many teachers, including Sonny Stokes and Bob Mandel. Then in San Diego, California, I learned about being more fully present as a therapist and as a vulnerable human being from Maurice Friedman, Viktor Frankl, Harold Bloomfield, Adelaide Bry, Wendy Piuck, Binnie Dansby, Sondra Ray, Linda Thistle, and Leonard Orr.

In Los Angeles, I have learned an enormous amount from many caring teachers, colleagues, and friends, including Rabbi Miriam Hamrell, Rabbi Mordecai Finley, Rabbi Ted Falcon, Rabbi Laura Geller, Rabbi Zalman Schachter-Shalomi, Janet Sternfeld Davis, Lucky Altman Lynch, Rabbi Harold Schulweis, Alan Morinis, Rabbi Marc Sirinsky and Catherine Coulson, Rabbi Sue Levi Elwell, Rabbi Marcia Plumb, Rabbi Stan Levy, Rabbi Brad Artson, Peter and Carol Reiss, Teri Bernstein, Rinat Amir, Janet Ruckert, Lynne Jacobs, Gary Yontef, Patricia Amrhein, Judy Schwimmer, Marion Klein, Ellen Dubois, Jean Katz,

Elaine Hall, Rabbi Jackie Redner, and many others in various havurot, musar classes, diverse congregations, and study groups that have been so helpful.

I would like to thank my inspiring and supportive literary agent, Stephanie Tade, who helped this book find its way to the world. I am extremely grateful to everyone at Trumpeter/Shambhala/Random House for their professionalism and kindness in guiding this project, especially the excellent editorial suggestions and support of Beth Frankl and Katie Keach.

Many family members have helped me reach this moment, including my loving parents, Martin and Ena Felder; my siblings, Janice Ruff, Andi Bittker, Ruthe Wagner, and Ron Wagner; and my mother, Helen Rothenberg Felder, of blessed memory. I am also grateful to my wife's family for all its support and kindness, especially June and Bill Schorin, Jeff Schorin, and the entire Wilstein family.

Tremendous love and support have come from my wife and best friend, Linda Schorin, and our amazing and creative son, Steven Alon Schorin Felder. It has been wonderful to study together, discuss these topics together, and journey through life together.

Most of all, I want to thank the mysterious Eternal One, the Creative Source that not only sparks these ideas but also gives the strength and direction to bring them to fruition. Each day of my life, no matter how stressful, is another chance to say thank you to the One who is so patient and loving.

Notes and Sources

INTRODUCTION

1. Dr. Viktor Frankl's books include *Man's Search for Meaning* (New York: Pocket, 1959); *The Doctor and the Soul* (New York: Bantam, 1969); and his autobiography, *Recollections* (New York: Basic Books, 2000).

2. Many Jewish teachings say that we should not try to limit God. For example, in *Sacred Fragments* (Philadelphia and Jerusalem: Jewish Publication Society, 1980), Rabbi Neil Gilman of the Jewish Theological Seminary in New York writes, "The cardinal theological sin for Heschel, then, is literal-mindedness, the presumption that our theological concepts are literally true or objectively adequate. . . . God is totally beyond human conceptualization. The most we can have are intimations of His Presence, an awareness of His reality." In the twelfth century, Rambam (Maimonides) said, "God should not be compared to anything else that exists, but as the universal Source of knowing" (*Guide for the Perplexed,* book 3, ch. 28). And the Talmud Tractate Hagigah 5b says, "God has a special and secret place where He resides and its name is *mistarim* (mystery). There is no access to the ultimate nature and secret of God. Still, God is close enough to describe with praises and attributes."

3. Regarding the fact that Jews are encouraged to question dogmatic teachers, in *The Essential Talmud* (New York: Bantam, 1977), Rabbi Adin Steinsaltz writes, "The student is expected

to pose questions to himself and others, and to voice doubts and reservations. The Talmud is perhaps the only sacred book in all of world culture that permits and even encourages the student to question it." The Talmud Tractate Avodah Zarah 190 advises, "Whoever learns from only one teacher will never have success." And Rabbi David Hartman of the Shalom Hartman Center in Jerusalem has said, "Judaism survives because it allows for many diverse and bold interpretations of the text. The eternal Voice out of Sinai is heard differently in each generation." From a June 2, 2007 interview online at The Shalom Hartman Institute.

CHAPTER I

1. The debate started with anthropologist Franz Boas in *The Handbook of North American Indians* (Washington, D.C.: Smithsonian, Bureau of American Ethnology, 1911). Then Benjamin Whorf cited it in *Language, Thought, and Reality* (Cambridge, Mass.: MIT Press, 1956), and Geoffrey Pullum questioned it in *The Great Eskimo Vocabulary Hoax* (Chicago: University of Chicago Press, 1991). There is also a middle position offered by Steven Jacobson in *Yup'ik Eskimo Dictionary* (Fairbanks, Alaska: Alaska Native Language Center, 1984).
2. Genesis 3:9–10.
3. See Norman Cohen, *Hineini in Our Lives* (Woodstock, Vt.: Jewish Lights, 2003)..
4. Paul Maclean, of the National Institute of Mental Health in Washington, D.C., described the triune theory of the brain in his book *The Triune Brain in Evolution* (New York: Springer, 1990).
5. Mario Beauregard, *The Spiritual Brain* (New York: HarperOne, 2007).
6. Andrew Newberg and Mark Robert Waldman, *How God Changes Your Brain* (New York: Ballantine, 2009); and Andrew Newberg, Eugene D'Aquili, and Vince Rause, *Why God Won't Go Away* (New York: Ballantine, 2002).

7. Daniel Siegel, *The Mindful Brain* (New York: Norton, 2007).
8. Jonah, Chapters 1–4.

CHAPTER 2

1. For more information about the Zeigarnik effect, see A. V. Zeigarnik, "Bluma Zeigarnik: A Memoir," *Gestalt Theory* 29, no. 3 (2007): 256–268; the original article, "Uberdas Behalten von erledigten und underledigten Handlungen," published in *Psychologische Forschung,* 1927; or the English summary in Willis Ellis, *A Source Book of Gestalt Psychology* (New York: Harcourt, 1938).
2. John Gottman, *The Seven Principles for Making Marriage Work* (New York: Crown, 1999), 42–44; Elizabeth Kensinger, *Emotional Memory Across the Adult Lifespan* (East Sussex, U.K.: Psychology Press, 2008).
3. Nosson Scherman, trans., *The Complete Artscroll Siddur* (Brooklyn, N.Y.: Mesorah, 1990), 58.
4. For more about Radical Amazement, see A. J. Heschel, *God in Search of Man: A Philosophy of Judaism* (New York: Farrar, Straus and Giroux, 1976); A. J. Heschel, *Man Is Not Alone* (New York: Farrar, Straus and Giroux, 1976); or Edward Kaplan, *Abraham Joshua Heschel: Prophetic Wisdom and Spiritual Radical* (New Haven, Conn.: Yale, 2009).
5. Aryeh Kaplan, *Jewish Meditation: A Practical Guide* (New York: Schocken, 1985), 93.
6. The tradition of one hundred blessings a day is found in Talmud Tractate Menachot 43b and is based on Deuteronomy 10:12—"Now Israel, what does Mah your God ask of you?" because the Hebrew word *me'ah,* meaning "one hundred," is close to *mah,* meaning "what."
7. The tradition of thirty-six blessings a day is based on double Chai (the word for life is *Chai* and its letters have the numerical equilavent of 18, so double Chai is 2 x 18 = 36).
8. For more on the scientific details of the Challenger errors, see Malcolm McConnell, *Challenger: A Major Malfunction* (New

York: Doubleday, 1987); or the Committee on Science and Technology, *Investigation of the Challenger Accident* (Washington, D.C.: Government Printing Office, 1986), http://www.gpoaccess.gov/challenger/64_420.pdf.

9. Shefa (or flow) is described in Sefer Yetzirah in the Kabbalah; Joseph Dan, *Kabbalah: A Very Short Introduction* (New York: Oxford University Press, 2006), 54–55; and Rabbi Asher ben David, *Perush Shem ha-Meforash*, edited by M. Chasida in *Ha-Segulah* nos. 2–10 (Jerusalem, 1934), 10, as quoted by Gershom Scholem, *On the Mystical Shape of the Godhead* (New York: Schocken, 1991), 108–109.

10. Marcia Falk, personal communications with author, 1984–85; and Marcia Falk, *The Book of Blessings* (New York: HarperCollins, 1996).

11. For more information about some of these studies, see Martin Seligman, *Learned Optimism* (New York: Vintage, 2006); Harold Koenig, *Medicine, Religion and Health: Where Science and Spirituality Meet* (West Conshohocken, Pa.: Templeton Press, 2008); and David Clark, Nash Boutros, and Mario Mendez, *The Brain and Behavior* (London: Cambridge University Press, 2010).

12. 1 Samuel 1:10–16.

CHAPTER 3

1. Macy Nulman, *Encyclopedia of Jewish Prayer* (Northvale, N.J.: Jason Aronson, 1993), 42. Talmud Tractate Berachot 60b says Asher Yatzar was recited twenty-four hundred years ago in the Great Assembly.

2. Descriptions of *kavanah* can be found in Micah 6:6–8; Psalms 51:15–17; Deuteronomy 30:6; several teachings of Rabbi Nachman of Bratslav (Aryeh Kaplan, *Rabbi Nachman's Wisdom,* Jerusalem: Breslov Institute, 1973); and Talmud Tractate Sanhedrin 106b.

3. Leviticus Rabbah 34:3.

4. Maimonides, "Laws Concerning Moral Dispositions and Ethical Conduct," *The Code of Maimonides* 4:1.

5. Before trying the exercises on any of the following DVDs, please consult with your physician or physical therapist about safety concerns and what is appropriate for your particular situation. Some DVDs that have worked for my clients with limited mobility are Amanda Cook, *Chair Workouts for Everyone—Wheelchair Workout* (2009); Nikki Glazer, *Chair Aerobics for Everyone* (2006); and Anne Burrell, *The Stronger Seniors Exercise Program* (2007).

6. For different views on the yetzer ha'ra and how to deal with it, see Moshe Chaim Luzatto, *The Way of God,* trans. Aryeh Kaplan (Jerusalem: Feldheim, 1997); David Fohrman, *The Beast That Crouches at the Door* (Englewood, N.J.: Devora, 2007); or Jay Michaelson, *God in Your Body: Kabbalah, Mindfulness, and Embodied Spiritual Direction* (Woodstock, Vt.: Jewish Lights, 2006).

7. See Talmud Tractate Berachot 34b, which says, "There is a holy place where only the person who has missed the mark can stand," and Deuteronomy 10:12–16, which says, "What does God ask of you? . . . circumcise your hearts." In other words, we are not separate or cut off from the Divine Presence when we are broken or struggling, but rather we may be in an open and receptive place where positive healing and reconnection can begin.

CHAPTER 4

1. Many resources are available to explain the concept of tzimtzum and the teachings of Rabbi Isaac Luria in detail. Some are Sanford Drob, *Symbols of the Kabbalah* (Northvale, N.J.: Jason Aronson, 2000); Sanford Drob, *Kabbalistic Metaphors* (Northvale, N.J.: Jason Aronson, 2001); Jacob Immanuel Schochet, *Mystical Concepts in Chasidism* (Brooklyn, N.Y.: Keter, 1979); Aryeh Kaplan, "Paradoxes," in *The Aryeh Kaplan Reader* (Brooklyn,

N.Y.: Artscroll, 1983); and Rachel Elior, "Tzimtzum: A Kabbalistic Approach to Creation," *Shema,* January 2010.

2. Similarities between Luria's teachings and the big bang theory are discussed in Daniel Matt, *God and the Big Bang* (Woodstock, Vt.: Jewish Lights, 1998); and Howard Smith, *Let There Be Light: Modern Cosmology and Kabbalah* (Novato, Calif.: New World Library, 2006).

3. Similarities between Luria's teachings and the theory of dark matter are discussed in Smith, *Let There Be Light.*

4. Iain Nicholson, *Dark Matter* (Baltimore, Md.: Johns Hopkins Press, 2007).

5. Similarities between the tzimtzum method and biofeedback training are discussed in Barbara Peavey, G. Frank Lawlis, and Arthur Goven, "Biofeedback-Assisted Relaxation," *Journal of Applied Psychophysiology* 10, no. 1 (March 1985); and Christine Craggs-Hinton, *How to Beat Pain* (London, U.K.: Sheldon Press, 2006).

CHAPTER 5

1. Various versions of the Pirke Avot are available, including Leonard Kravitz and Kerry M. Olitzky, eds. and trans., *Pirke Avot: A Modern Commentary on Jewish Ethics* (New York: UAHC Press, 1993); and Moshe Lieber, *The Pirkei Avos Treasury: Ethics of the Fathers: The Sages' Guide to Living with an Anthologized Commentary and Anecdotes* (Brooklyn, N.Y.: Artscroll, 1995).

2. Pirke Avot 4:1.

3. For more details on such research, see Arnold Beiser, "The Paradoxical Theory of Change," in *Gestalt Therapy Now,* ed. Joen Fagan and Irma Lee Shepherd (New York: Harper, 1970), 77–80; and Marsha Linehan, *Skills Training Manual for Treating Borderline Personality Disorder* (New York: Guilford, 1993).

4. Searching for the hidden spark of holy light is explained in David Cooper, *God Is a Verb* (New York: Riverhead, 1997);

and Yitzhak Buxbaum, *Jewish Spiritual Practices* (Northvale, N.J.: Jason Aronson, 1990), 215.

CHAPTER 6

1. The phrase "Gam zu L'tovah" can be found in Masseches Ta'anis 21a; and Arthur Kurzweil, *Kabbalah for Dummies* (New York: Hungry Minds, 2006).
2. For more information about Rabbi Akiva, see Joseph Telushkin, *Jewish Literacy* (New York: William Morrow, 1991); and Meir Lehmann and Pearly Zucker, *Akiva* (Jerusalem: Feldheim, 2003).
3. See the books cited in note 1 for the Introduction: *Man's Search for Meaning, The Doctor and the Soul,* and *Recollections.*
4. For more about this theory, see Sanford Drob, *Kabbalistic Metaphors* (Northvale, N.J.: Jason Aronson, 2001); and Donald Wilder Menzi and Zwe Padeh, trans., *The Tree of Life: Chayyim Vital's Introduction to the Kabbalah of Isaac Luria* (New York: Arizal Publications, 2008).
5. Harold Schulweis, "Was God in the Earthquake?" *Jewish Journal of Los Angeles,* January 24, 1994, http://www.vbs.org/rabbi/hshulw/earth.htm.
6. This theory is explained in Ira Robinson, *Moses Cordovero's Introduction to Kabbalah* (New York: Yeshiva University, 1994); and Menzi and Padeh, trans., *The Tree of Life.*
7. Talmud Tractate Berachot 59b. See also the teachings of Rabbi Zundel (the mentor of Rabbi Israel Salanter, who founded the Musar movement of character development). Rabbi Zundel spoke about the need to bless not only the good that happens to us but also the misfortunes in *Rabbi Israel Mi-Salant, MiDor l'Dor,* ed. Rabbi Dov Katz, vol. 2 (Jerusalem: Ha-Histadrut ha-Tzionit ha-Olamit, 10), as cited in Yitzhak Buxbaum, *Jewish Spiritual Practices* (Northvale, N.J.: Jason Aronson, 1990), 624–625.
8. The Baal Shem Tov discusses the journey of a soul who comes to this life and dies young to complete an earlier purpose; this

discussion is cited in Shmuel Boteach, *Wrestling with the Divine: A Jewish Response to Suffering* (Northvale, N.J.: Jason Aronson, 1995), 154–156. Many Talmud scholars point to the story of Beruriah and her husband, Rabbi Meir, who lost two sons. Beruriah described it as "a Visitor who reclaimed what belonged to Him," as cited in Yalkut Proverbs 964. In addition, see Maurice Lamm, *The Jewish Way in Death and Mourning* (New York: Jonathan David Publishers, 2000); and Neal Goldberg and Miriam Liebermann, *Saying Goodbye* (Southfield, Mich.: Targum Press, 2004).

9. For more about expressing anger at God, see Solomon Schimmel, *Wounds Not Healed by Time* (New York: Oxford University Press, 2002), 134–40; and Harold Schulweis, *For Those Who Can't Believe: Overcoming the Obstacles to Faith* (New York: HarperCollins, 1994), 84–85.

10. See the third paragraph of the Kaddish prayer.

11. Harold Kushner, *When Bad Things Happen to Good People* (New York: Schocken, 1981), 147-48, 154.

12. Process theology is discussed in Sandra Lubarsky and David Ray Griffin, *Jewish Theology and Process Thought* (Albany, N.Y.: State University of New York Press, 1995); and Bradley Shavit Artson, "Ba-Derekh: On the Way—A Presentation of Process Theology," 2008 podcast, Center for Process Studies, http://www.ctr4process.org/media or www.newcaje.org/40029.pdf.

13. Julie Gruenbaum Fax, "Community," *Jewish Journal of Greater Los Angeles*, March 5–11, 2010.

14. 1 Kings 19:12.

CHAPTER 7

1. Attention deficit disorder is described in Edward Hallowell and John Ratey, *Delivered from Distraction* (New York: Ballantine, 2005); and Edward Hallowell and Peter Jensen, *Superparenting for ADD* (New York: Ballantine, 2010).

2. Talmud Tractate Shabbat 127a and Talmud Berachot 60b.

3. For more information on the diverse and fascinating concepts of soul-connected life after physical death that have been explored in Judaism for many centuries, please pick up the comprehensive book *Jewish Views of the Afterlife* by Simcha Paul Raphael (Northvale, N.J.: Jason Aronson, 1994).

4. For more information about the debate over whether or not the moon and tides actually affect our bodies, see Ivan Kelly, James Rotton, and Roger Culver, "The Moon Was Full and Nothing Happened," in *The Outer Edge* (Amherst, N.Y.: CSICOP, 1996); Arnold Lieber, *How the Moon Affects You* (New York: Dell, 1980); and Lori-Ann Parker, *At the Feet of the Moon* (Frederick, Md.: Publish America, 2006).

5. To explore research on interconnectedness, see George Leonard, *The Silent Pulse* (New York: Plume, 1978).

CHAPTER 8

1. For additional uses of the Shehecheyanu phrase, see Talmud Tractates Berakhot 54a, Pesachim 7b, and Sukkah 46a.

2. The concept of beginner's mind is explained in Shunryu Suzuki, *Zen Mind, Beginner's Mind* (Boston, Mass.: Weatherhill, 1973).

3. For examples of such studies, see William Fezler, *Creative Imagery: How to Visualize in All Five Senses* (New York: Simon and Schuster, 1989); or Ronald Finke, *Creative Imagery: Discoveries and Inventions in Visualization* (New York: Routledge, 1990).

4. Thomas Kuhn, *The Structure of Scientific Revolutions* (Chicago: University of Chicago Press, 1962).

5. Jerome Bruner and Leo Postman, "On the Perception of Incongruity: A Paradigm," *Journal of Personality* 18 (1949): 206–223.

6. See Exodus 3:14, Talmud Tractate Baba Bathra 73a, Talmud Tractate Berachot 9b, and Talmud Tractate Shevuot 35a; and K. J. Cronin, "The Name of God Is Revealed in Exodus 3:14" at http://www.exodus-314.com.

About the Author

Leonard Felder, PhD, is a licensed psychologist in West Los Angeles. He has written twelve books on Jewish spirituality and personal growth that have sold more than one million copies and have been translated into fourteen languages. These titles include *Seven Prayers That Can Change Your Life, The Ten Challenges, When Difficult Relatives Happen to Good People, Fitting In Is Overrated, Wake Up or Break Up,* and *Making Peace with Your Parents.*

He has been invited to lead discussions on the connection between Jewish texts and daily psychological dilemmas at thirty-five temples and synagogues, fourteen Jewish book fairs, plus dozens of churches and interfaith events nationwide. He has also appeared on more than two hundred radio and television programs, including *Oprah, The Today Show,* CNN, *The CBS Early Show, NBC Nightly News,* National Public Radio, Canada AM, and BBC London.

Active in several volunteer organizations, he received the Distinguished Merit Citation of the National Conference of Community and Justice for developing innovative programs to combat racism, sexism, homophobia, and religious prejudice. Dr. Felder's books have also received numerous national awards, including the 1985 Nonfiction Book of the Year Award from *Medical Self-Care* magazine, Best Jewish Writing 2002 from Jossey-Bass, 2008 Nonfiction Book of the Year from *Body and Soul* magazine, and one of 2008's Best Five Psychology Books from The Books for a Better Life Foundation in New York.

Originally from Detroit, Michigan, Dr. Felder graduated with high honors from Kenyon College in Ohio and worked in New York as the director of research for Doubleday and Company before completing his PhD in psychology and becoming a therapist in Los Angeles. He and his wife, Linda Schorin, a visual artist, live in Mar Vista, California, with their son, Steven.

Discussion Guide

These questions and guidelines can be used as a one-session, two-session, four-session, or eight-session group discussion or class. They can also be used as a two-person weekly or monthly conversation with a study partner, or as a solo exploration of these topics.

Please appreciate that each person will have different and completely valid answers to these questions. By respecting each person's unique ideas and experiences, we can learn from one another without requiring one fixed way of believing or practicing.

May these questions and conversations help you and your loved ones to go deeper into Jewish spiritual wisdom regarding how to live each day with even more love, health, creativity, insight, and courage.

CHAPTER 1: A RECENTERING METHOD FOR ANY STRESSFUL MOMENT

(Please choose two or more of the following.)

1. What do you define as "too little stress," "too much stress," or "just the right amount of challenge" on a given week?
2. What are the moments in your life currently when you feel most rushed, overloaded, pulled in opposing directions, or knocked off center?
3. What have you found to be useful, or not very useful, for regaining your center and your clarity during an especially tense or upsetting moment?

4. When you have experimented with the calm breathing, the "Where Are You?" question, and the "Hineini. Here I Am" phrases discussed in chapter 1, what did you notice about your eyesight, your clarity of mind, your energy, or your ability to be more present and compassionate? Did it work for you right away or did it take repeated practice?

5. As a child, were you taught that a conversation with the Divine Presence or with the "still, small voice within" can help you stay centered? If so, what were you taught?

6. What do you currently believe, or not believe, about how to align yourself with the Source of Life?

7. What are the obstacles, distractions, and habits that make it harder for you to connect with your strong, pure center? What might be your next steps for moving forward on the journey to a more genuine and alive sense of "Hineini. Here I Am"?

CHAPTER 2: OUTSMARTING THE ANXIOUS, MOODY BRAIN

(Please choose two or more of the following.)

1. In chapter 2 we discussed the Zeigarnik effect, the idea that the human brain is more interested in problems and doesn't tend to notice or absorb what's going right or what has positive possibilities. When have you experienced the Zeigarnik effect?

2. Do you find that hyper-vigilance or problem-seeking ability is beneficial in one area of your life, but causes friction in another area of your life?

3. When have you experienced Rabbi Abraham Joshua Heschel's moments of "Radical Amazement"? What is your particular way of noticing and taking to heart the beauty, the blessings, the small triumphs, and the mysteries of life? What is your favorite method or phrase for saying "thank you" to the Source of Life, or for feeling re-energized on a busy day?

Do you prefer a consistent way of expressing gratitude and awareness, or do you prefer a spontaneous response?

4. When you are in a prayer service or a spiritual gathering, do you tend to connect with the words that praise and thank a mysterious Source, or do you struggle with those words and ideas?

5. What tends to cause you to feel more or less grateful? What are the moments when your mind reverts to seeing what's missing or frustrating? When do you notice that which is positive and nourishing around you and within you?

CHAPTER 3: BECOMING HEALTHIER SO YOU CAN DEAL WITH STRESSFUL DAYS

(Please choose two or more of the following.)

1. When have you or a loved one experienced a blockage of some crucial physical or energetic flow in your body, and how did you attempt to resolve the problem?

2. What were you taught and what do you currently believe (or not believe) about the possible connection between your thoughts, your daily actions, and your health?

3. What, if anything, would you change about your eating habits, your water intake, your relationship to exercise, or your way of dealing with stress if you were to have a moment of conversation each day with the Source (whatever you believe that Source to be) who gave you this vulnerable and intricate body?

4. What is the one habit or behavior that is hardest for you to change with regard to your health or vitality? (Please keep all answers confidential and private within the group, or work on this question silently.)

5. What kind of additional support, reminders, or next steps will help you take better care of the gift of life that has been entrusted to you?

CHAPTER 4: DISCOVERING WHEN TO INTERVENE AND WHEN TO LET GO

(Please choose two or more of the following.)

1. What have been your most satisfying and most frustrating experiences when trying to delegate to others, or encouraging others to lighten your load?

2. When do you tend to give up too much control or be too trusting, and then feel let down by the results?

3. When do you tend to exert too much control or micromanage? When has that caused someone to do less than he or she could be doing, or to resent you?

4. What would your daily life be like if you could hold on to the tasks you want to do in your own style, but let go of other tasks that others could do with minimum guidance from you?

5. How do you feel about the mystical idea of tzimtzum, or a Creative Source pulling back somewhat in order to allow for free will, partnership, and spontaneity in life?

6. If you used the idea of tzimtzum, how might it improve your family relationships, your work life, or your volunteer teamwork?

CHAPTER 5: RESPONDING WITH WISDOM WHEN SOMEONE TREATS YOU HARSHLY

(Please choose two or more of the following.)

1. Is there a particular behavior or character trait (in yourself or others) that causes you to feel impatient, upset, judgmental, or intolerant?

2. Is there a situation in your life in which someone seems to be draining your energy, blocking your best efforts, or getting on your nerves? (Please talk about the behavior rather than the person's name or anything that might reveal their identity.)

3. What do you think might be the possible benefit of the Pirke Avot statement in chapter 5 that "the wise person is the one who learns from each human being"? What might be the

hidden benefit of your interactions with the person or people who came to mind earlier? For example, is this person giving you much-needed practice on how be firm and compassionate when dealing with a difficult individual?

4. When you think about this person who gets on your nerves, is there any possibility that this individual might be offering you a clear picture of who you don't want to be? Is it possible to learn a lot about what you want to do, or not do, by studying this person's actions and the impact he or she has on others?

5. Could there be a hidden or diminished part of yourself that this other person has in excess? For example, what irritating quality does this person exhibit beyond what is tolerable, and yet you have been so afraid to exhibit any of that same character trait that it has been costing you in certain situations? What would happen if you found a decent and appropriate way to exhibit just a little of the quality that you have been suppressing (without becoming irritating like this other person tends to be)?

CHAPTER 6: BEING OPEN TO A HIDDEN GIFT IN THE MOST DISTRESSING MOMENTS

(Please choose two or more of the following.)

1. In the past, have you been given a "Jewish explanation" for why tragedies and traumas happen to good people? What have you been told?

2. Which of the several Jewish teachings in chapter 6 seems to you to be the most or least likely spiritual explanation for why painful things happen to decent people?

3. When would you feel comforted and guided by the phrase "Gam zu l'tovah. Even this might someday become for the good," and when would you feel hurt or upset as a result of someone saying these words to you?

4. What painful event, loss, or trauma in your own life have you somehow managed to turn into something insightful, healing, or positive?

5. What hurt, loss, or trauma in your own life still feels unresolved and in need of some small or large *tikkun,* or repair, that might prevent future suffering for yourself or others?

CHAPTER 7: FINDING THE QUIET, PEACEFUL PLACE BENEATH THE AGITATION

(Please choose two or more of the following.)

1. What is your way of envisioning the Jewish idea of a "pure soul," and what do you currently believe (or not believe) about the existence of a spark of holiness or goodness within each human being?
2. When have you found it difficult (and when have you found it easy) to reach a level of deep inner calm and peacefulness on a stressful day?
3. What tends to be the habit, distraction, or numbing escape that sometimes causes you to forget or lose touch with the pure soul that is deep within you? (Please keep all answers confidential and private within the group, or work on this question silently.)
4. When you have experimented with the "Elohai n'shamah" prayer during a challenging moment, what have you noticed about your internal state of being?
5. In the next few days or weeks, what kind of reminder would you like to utilize on a busy day to help you connect with your pure soul?

CHAPTER 8: SEEING NEW POSSIBILITIES IN EACH MOMENT

(Please choose two or more of the following.)

1. What moments in your life have started to feel repetitive, uninspiring, or no longer as interesting as they once were?
2. What do you experience when you use the blessing in chapter 8 to open up to a new way of seeing in these particular mo-

ments? Do the moments stay the same or do they turn into something different with these words in mind?

3. What are some recent moments in your life when you've felt a sense of newness, curiosity, vitality, or spontaneity?

4. What do you experience if you use the blessing in chapter 8 to boost those particular moments? Do the moments have an added depth or joy when you say these particular words?

5. When you are doing something creative or trying to come up with an innovative solution to a dilemma, do you ever stop and say a prayer or a meditation for seeing the issue with new eyes and a new perspective?

6. What do you notice about yourself and your approach to a dilemma when you use this method?

7. Are there moments you share with the people you care about, or activities that you enjoy, that might be enhanced by saying specific words that boost your creative openness? What are those moments?